Philosophy of the Center of Civilization

Established January 2024

New York, NY

United States of America

© 2024 Baruch Menache

All rights reserved.

Published by McWest & Associates

ISBN: 978-1-971928-14-2

Philosophy of the Center of Civilization

Baruch Menache

The Nature of Intimacy in Philosophy and Culture 25

The Universal Center – Consciousness and Biology 33

Consciousness - Physical Realm 39

The Paradox of Reflection and Existence 43

Alcohol and the Rearrangement of the Psyche 51

Identities in the Centric Locale 63

The Domestication in the Center Locality 73

On Strangers and Social Interaction

Outskirts: Idealized Domestication, Public Intimacy, and Political Reality

Part 2: 113

The Interactive Embodied Environment: Psychic Parts and Domesticative systems. 115

The Interactive Locale— Exhausted Data Center 121

The Role of Therapeutic Properties in Integrative Healing

Contextual Frameworks and Regulation of Interaction within the Domestic locale

Part 1:

The Centric Locale and the Illusion of Boundlessness

We must analyze the primary features and elucidate the experiential philosophy inherent in the centric locale. The text suggests the existence of a conglomerate that constitutes a performative system, situated within an unlimited expanse. Participants, characterized by their privilege, posit that the system is sufficiently extensive as to defy association with any finite structure. Within this framework, a significant transgression is considered to be the revelation of the inherent limitations of both its citizens and broader conceptualization of society. Indeed, referring to it as a society may be regarded as a problematic overgeneralization; rather, it may be more appropriate to designate it as an idea, a mistake, a concept, a perspective, or even a delinquency—rather than categorizing it as a society among societies—in order to allow its classification to evolve over time.

Medical Stigma and the Fear of Mortality

This approach offers an explanation for the stigma associated with one's medical history, given that medical privacy is regarded as a sacrosanct value across all locales. The devaluation of an individual's identity is considered less significant than the exposure of the human condition to the rigorous scrutiny inherent in medical practice. Such stigma implies a preference for perceiving the collective as possessing an enduring, almost immortal character, thereby preventing the individual from undermining that perception with the reality of mortality—particularly in light of the singular nature of the experience of death. This phenomenon illustrates a failure to engage fully with a life instilled with importance. This perspective may rule all classes, remaining unwilling to notice the margins of any person, idea, institution, or structure.

Relational Personhood and the Limits of Recognition

Personhood is not defined solely by the span of a lifetime; rather, it is a relational entity—part of a larger system that does not terminate, at least not in any foreseeable future. What matters for our inquiry is not a person's biological makeup but how they relate to public relationships. These can be contrasted with private relationships—which do not attract the notice of the collective and are not considered imperative. The only relationships that can be resolved as part of a collective study are those that can be discussed and scrutinized, having been granted the right to be observed. Those that do not meet these criteria are neither known, represented, nor examined; they are simply viewed as non-existent within collective consciousness.

Domestic legality is reserved for relationships deemed to warrant bureaucratic scrutiny, and thus judgment is not extended to those of seemingly lesser legal status that would not attract bureaucratic attention.

We tend to dismiss the aspect of culture that fixates on a person's actions as merely a byproduct of an entrepreneurial mindset. In doing so, we overlook a deeper analysis that reveals our concern for individuals is largely contingent on their relatability to us.

As a result, it is not unusual for a person's actions to exist independently of the market system, yet this often provokes a sense of envy from onlookers. This envy arises from the fact that some individuals manage to remain fully engaged with their pursuits, maintaining an unbroken relationship with their work, even in the face of market pressures. Observing this, we do not ask ourselves how to pursue our true passions despite market constraints; rather, we wonder how to carry out our existing roles in a way that fosters a profounder joining, one that transcends market-driven imperatives.

The Infinite Relationship: Beyond Romantic Idealism

The reason the relational aspect is so recognized, despite its distance from theory, is not for the sake of weightier experience, as might be the case for romantics, but because of the extent that it conveys. To be in an absolute relationship with something or someone also means having an inexhaustible perspective upon the situation. For we can never find a moment or experience that might be called the end, as it always relates to another moment or experience. It is endless—not in the romantic sense, but on an advanced level—one of reality itself, devoid of a finish line.

Therefore, the entire relational notion in this philosophy is tied to the unlimited expanse being sought. We can deduce this because, when tested, the unlimited expanse stands out as the defining aspect.

However, if a relationship is about to terminate, we would seek to engage with the course of the conclusion, ensuring that its deduction remains evocative. We would venerate those final moments as necessary to move on, yet recognize them as intensely effective. Instead of relating solely to the immense history of the relationship and thus questioning the termination process, we would want to ensure that we are never in a situation where we cannot engage with the final moments by extending the experience. In this way, we would rather use those last moments of energy to gain an experience of separation—thus allowing the relationship to continue in its termination—than expend efforts reflecting on the relationship as a whole and risk a quick, unrelatable end.

This is also the rationale behind certain morbid ideas, which begin to elevate the notion of death so that, when that moment comes, it becomes completely relatable. Instead of spending more on relating to notions of life, they seek the unlimited expanse of relating to their death. For if life remains the focus, then death may arrive unpredictably, making life itself seem incomplete or constrained. This desire may be so profound that one might bring about one's demise in a manner that aligns with one's worldview, e.g., self-sabotage. Such is the case for one who would rather experience the unlimited expanse than face the fear of possible emptiness ascending from existence. However, this is a terminal case—one taken to extremes, as are many philosophies that have been taken to extremes.

Consider a prominent idea or philosophy that arises within intellectual or political spheres after a major societal shift. Although it may appear straightforward, the depth and practical implications of such an idea often present challenges to its full integration within various social contexts. Once adopted into dominant discourse, however, the idea tends to endure, as removing it could reveal limitations within that social framework.

To prevent the concept from appearing finite, societies often employ it in diverse contexts that extend beyond its original tenets. While these applications may not entirely align with the core philosophy, they allow the idea to persist by adapting it to contemporary circumstances. If one were to critique any ideological perspective—say, as a philosophy that bridges abstract ideas with practical life—dismissing it entirely would ignore the significant overlap between philosophical ideas and lived reality. Thus, ideologies are often retained in an adapted form—not necessarily as pure ideology but as part of a cultural dialogue that resists absolute boundaries.

When dominant cultures react to ideological movements by labeling individuals as adherents of a particular ideology, they may effectively sideline those individuals without directly confronting the underlying ideas. This tactic—branding people within specific ideological categories—allows society to protect its intellectual landscape from perceived disruption. Yet rather than diminishing the idea's influence, this labeling reflects a cultural impulse to absorb diverse perspectives without wholly integrating them, allowing the ideology to exist as a manageable part of an "unlimited expanse" rather than as a finite concept with clear limits.

The only way to deal with ideas without entrenching them into fixed identities is to make them relatable to other ideas. For instance, with certain ideologies we can acknowledge that all political action has roots in prior philosophies —and that further inquiry involves seeking out those heritages. This approach would allow us to eliminate the notion of practical philosophy as an isolated idea within broader society. Suffice it to say, it will continue as a means to uncover the philosophical structure of politics, as Aristotle set out to do.

To perform such a task, we must fully immerse in the concept, uncertain whether we will be influenced by its domain. Then, after being within the idea, we can reach out to other ideas which may relate to it. We do so only because ideas do not last forever; only their relationships do. That is, unless an extinction event occurs—which, we can argue, will still leave traces of the past that relate to the present moment. The elements that do not reach into the future in any relatable fashion, still contribute relational material to the chain.

We cannot even conceive an element, idea, or person not participating in this chain, for every idea, entity, or person inevitably connects to something else within our cognitive framework. Thought processes cannot occur towards an unrelatable aspect because of their inherent need to relate to what is being followed. When we assert that something is unrelatable, we are demonstrating a difficulty in unearthing its relation. We do not have a word for something that cannot be related on any level of analysis, as this would be impossible.

The scenario of an extinction event is an objective situation—one that does not account for the subjective state within it. When we enter into the subjective experience of extinction (which is not conceivable), there is no such thing as being unrelatable. The objective notion of the extinction event is relatable because we are speaking of it. This concept connects too many things, such as the experience of loss regarding the relational material between an individual and an object. Although there is a thread of relational material accessible in certain environments, according to the subjective experience it seems like a non-relationship. Therefore, the extinction event relates to those experiences of a seemingly non-relationship and consequently to emptiness.

Had an individual developed an awareness of this fact, the extinction event would seem less and less relatable. Thus, there were entire societies that could not even muster the mental capabilities to grasp the notion of an extinction event. The contemporary awareness is a new development within the imagination but still a mistaken assumption of claiming non-relationship material to be an absolute reality.

The Role of Relationships in Identity

In any idea, we would seek to understand its networks and investigate them in a way that reinforces the stability of that notion. Even ideas that appear precarious yet remain dynamic can—and should—be engaged under this centric philosophy, even at some risk, so that we may able to progress towards related concepts. This approach is the only viable way to manage overwhelming ideas within a philosophy that refuses to let them expire.

Thus, we begin to develop a formula for the breeding ground of ideologies within this centric framework. Ideas that seem determined do so largely because a significant portion of the inhabitants is unwilling to engage with their personal domain. Had they engaged with it, they would have transitioned to an interrelated domain, thereby diminishing the idea's momentum.

Although not every ideology exhibits this characteristic, in a philosophy that rejects the notion of limited ideas, such tendencies are common. Consequently, certain ideologies acquire a political dimension simply because the majority avoids engaging with them. By understanding these underlying explanations and their associations with other contexts, we may find solutions to historical conflicts.

Moreover, alternative paths may be necessary to avoid repeating previous patterns, and emerging philosophies often serve this purpose. Following major societal shifts, these new philosophies challenge established ideas in a general manner rather than on an individual basis. The risk involved may be considered too great, and thus such challenges are often politically avoided—even though the alternative might lead to a prolonged ordeal.

When significant shifts are desirable to prevent repeating former errors, societies may require to embrace new philosophies—even those that challenge prevailing discourse. Such shifts might be temporary, allowing networks with other ideas to persevere. However, during this interim, the risk is twofold: society jeopardies severing its bond with that never-ending expanse, and it may overemphasize engaging with new material despite the strength of existing ideas.

In these circumstances, a kind of "super-ego" is lost, leaving only the intrinsic value of human connections to drive engagement with new material. Even if the guiding philosophy is eventually abandoned, we can still cherish relationships and, despite the allure of any idea, strive to progress toward new ground. This responsibility falls to the romantics and to those who pursue connections regardless of theory. It is a risk that the populace cannot be sure to manage satisfactorily. Thus, people remain burdened with ideological baggage: they must either develop a new philosophy, such that distances itself from historical blunders or foster authentic human connection, namely familial, which facilitate evocative engagement with innovative ideas. Importantly, this process must be undertaken by the majority—not just by an elite group of intellectuals.

This issue can be resolved either through the adoption of a new philosophy or by establishing clear distinctions to guide the future. I believe that the relational aspect—trusting that relationships will deepen despite abstract representations—was a key factor in ending the era of the World Wars. Not through any grand narrative, but because those relational elements remained full-bodied on the battlefield; even as they contracted due to the effect of war, they did not disappear from its relational element, and neither did we. Popular battlefield films highlight the steadfast relationships that soldiers maintained in the face of death and war—often through humor or banter— unlike historical figures who merely operated within a system, one to transition to its next phase.

Thus, the challenge posed by certain ideologies can be addressed by emphasizing relationships, even in the face of abstract theories. Proponents of strong ideas or outstanding theories are inevitably channeled through relational frameworks, enabling them to enter and exit the political arena. Political stagnation often occurs when ideas lack relational value, leaving them overly active and overstimulated while the surrounding environment remains static. Then an idea may be assumed to be the foundation of reality, all without connecting to the other notions which constitute that reality. A key principle of centric philosophy is that "no reality is truly a reality despite our insistence upon it."

It is understandable to insist that reality is real, as one can experience events with a depth reserved for absolute experiences. Depth is what one pursues when affirming reality—much like a child who resists departing from the mother's breast. That experience carries a sense of absoluteness to which even adults can relate with concentrated nostalgia, while the child rejects any lesser form of absoluteness. Movements made outside the comfort of that experience are felt with less depth and intensity. This mode of experience does not change in adulthood, making it difficult to leave behind a version of reality that once offered an absolute experience akin to the mother's breast. Yet, once we discard the notion of any reality as absolute, we fully depart from that complexity.

Ironically, when we remove the notion of an absolute reality—one that always transcends the self—we may eventually experience absoluteness in all things. The child's movements after leaving the breast are perceived as less absolute only because the child cannot yet conceive that all of reality forms a cosmic whole. If the child could, even simple movements would be seen as absolute alongside the mother's breast. In fact, this diminished sense of absoluteness arises because the child internalizes the notion that what lies beyond the immediate environment is less interactive and realistic. If society consistently embraced the idea that everything beyond one's immediate experience is equally real, one would quickly attach to new experiences upon departing from any former state.

There exists a subjective attachment to certain realities that aligns with an objective framework. For the child, the mother's breast represents the ideal reality, though it depends on various facets of the experience to provide the consistency the child assumes to be absolute. Indeed, this assumption conflicts with a broader view of reality in which the mother's breast is merely one point on an endless continuum—extending to every movement the child makes after leaving it. Thus, absoluteness is available in all things, permitting the reproduction of the child's experience when a philosophy aligns accordingly.

However, the limitations of the human form—even within a never-ending expanse—introduce constraints. The human body is a complex construct with specific needs that render certain forms of reality more self-serving. The mother's breast appears absolute to the child because the child is bound by its physiological needs, and life and death remain absolute notions precisely because the body is inextricably linked to them.

The philosophy of the centric locale produces a populace that is less engaged with its experiences, thereby losing the sense of the "mother's breast." Within the never-ending expanse, no concrete framework emerges to shape experiences, as doing so would impose limiting boundaries. Relationships, being based solely on subjective views, do not establish absoluteness. When a smaller form of reality is subsumed by the expanse, every mode of reality is dismissed as a fool's errand.

Cynicism and the Rejection of Frameworks

This fosters a cynical view of any framework, since reality is always more than it appears. The populace focuses on what is objectively true or false; any reality aligned with current realist understandings—though connected to the expanse—is deemed true only momentarily. Even though such classifications merely frame reality without capturing its absolute nature, the philosophy permits human beings to adopt a reality while remaining willing to abandon it for the never-ending expanse.

One might assume that relationships could remedy the lack of absoluteness in this philosophy; however, as noted, they only serve to connect past experiences. They can evoke memories of the mother's breast, but they cannot fully reproduce that experience. Although relationships can deepen one's passions and lend them a sense of absoluteness, they do not generate the formula by which these passions arise. Thus, relationships can only complement a realistic framework—they cannot create it.

The solution lies in allowing every identity to thrive—hence the term "centric locale." Multiple identities within this overarching philosophy enable individuals to express themselves within private affairs while remaining connected to the never-ending expanse. New identities are not only permitted but actively encouraged. When a citizen lacks a secondary identity, they are regarded as questionable within this societal framework.

Clearly, this multiplicity creates conflict, as identities that serve as frameworks of certain reality naturally oppose one another, leading to divisions that undermine society. This issue is managed by admonishing the populace for becoming overly attached to their identities, which weakens their bond to a broader, less threatening collective. Identities accept certain political freedoms and compensate for their isolation by diminishing attachment to individual self.

Most identities accept this compromise; they advance some political autonomy while inherently opposing the political structure—which has the benefits of these identities to compensate for its lack of absoluteness. Because they inherently oppose one another, identities choose not to assume a prominent role in the political arena, allowing them to continue unabated. Constituents of an identity refrain from adhering with excessive intensity, adopting a detached attitude that, while it may not fundamentally matter, still commands respect. Therefore, there is no need to take a political stance because the identity is not recognized as an absolute form of reality—much less one deserving full exposure.

When a social group or perspective asserts a strong position, immediate pushback may diminish its perceived relevance through various social dynamics. Members are encouraged to adhere to certain parameters and perform routine tasks in service of society, thereby lessening their personal attachments. Other identities surround them as a silent demonstration, to which everyone coexists despite differences—even if occupied understanding is impossible. However, this creates animosity toward those who steadfastly sustain their identity, and such individuals may begin to feel shame for promoting their identity under society's banner, as if they were overlooking a larger reality.

Individuals can only maintain this stance briefly before the allure of a broader reality infiltrates their worldview, intensifying their shame, concluded by a detachment from wider social environments. Ultimately, only those identities that captivate the majority persist, leaving little incentive to weaken their attachments. In this context, bureaucracy is fine-tuned; individuals construct realistic frameworks while bureaucratic measures integrate them under a banner that encompasses many identities.

Thus, problematic identities must be isolated from anything associated with the centric locale, since such an association would connect to other integral realities. Isolation must occur at multiple levels—from bureaucratic measures to social environments, including locations and modes of travel. Officials in the centric locale avoid taking political action against these identities, as doing so would imply that they are a limited expanse, wary of certain forms.

Instead, the judicial body diligently seeks wrongdoing with determined intensity to undermine their morale. Even as it protects the expression of identity, it ties these identities to broader society to the point that they are viewed as lawbreakers. The courts identify troubling trends of isolation—a significant indicator of criminality—and demand communal attachments through measures such as imprisonment, community work, or therapeutic intervention.

The judicial body enforces the core tenets of the philosophy—or, more accurately, ensures that its structural flaws are remedied. Isolated identity is particularly problematic, as the never-ending expanse cannot account for its overall influence on citizens. Given that isolation is encouraged to mitigate the experience of absoluteness, the judicial body's primary concern is to promote community among the isolated and to weaken identities that are excessively rigid. Consequently, the populace's focus on criminality shifts to both the isolated criminal and the isolated identity. Criminals are dealt with harshly for not participating in communal dialogue, while identities are addressed by politicizing their high-profile cases until the populace is forced into both dialogue and opposition. This process creates sufficient social connection to isolated identities, rendering their folly evident.

This dynamic is illustrated by the public's attention to organized crime. The distinction between crime syndicates that attract attention is based on the complexity of their organizations: sophisticated groups intrigue a large portion of the populace, while simpler groups rarely garner media coverage. When criminality and organization combine, they capture public attention. Most identities in the centric locale can be characterized as organizations. When these identities form their own statehood, public interest is piqued as people become curious about their internal interactions and broader social relationships.

Exploring the Tension between Political Identity, Violence, and the Concept of an Unlimited Reality

A core philosophical question remains: How political can an identity become, and how would its interactions be maintained? The intrigue lies in its adherence to a standard of ethics even as it generates its own form of violence within an overarching political configuration. When a philosophy is conceived as a never-ending expanse and an identity is created which seems both absolute and politically potent, enough to provoke judicial action through violence, an ideal model of political philosophy is born.

All identities under this banner are dissatisfied with their lack of absoluteness and strive to expand and express themselves—even to the point of provoking judicial intervention. This key issue is not easily resolved, as such organizations ultimately become a menace to society, prompting the judicial body to undermine their morale. One effective tactic has been to turn these organizations against one another—producing evidence while simultaneously decimating their structure by rendering them subservient to the state's overarching framework. Even the act of denouncing a fellow member fosters mistrust and exposes that member's isolated identity to the broader world.

One might expect an increase in organized systems of dissent or resistance—both in reality and in representation—in a society where active political engagement is absent. Yet, there is a reminiscence for the times when such activities were more common, as if political engagement were once more widely shared. However, since philosophical needs persist, we must ask how these needs were met without a corresponding rise in identity-based political action.

Reminiscence for an era when identities actively engaged in political action also recalls a time when broader society was not perceived as a never-ending expanse. Prior to this, the philosophy focused on the expanse but included a caveat regarding which identities can best serve the political sphere rather than the overarching system. In other words, the experience of absoluteness once outweighed the notion of a never-ending expanse.

This duality—either in its infancy or later reversed—placed the framework of reality above reality itself. Those who seem sentimental recall the certainty of one's place in the world—a certainty that, when questioned, would have immediately provoked violent action. This represents an immature version of what has evolved into the present day: the "mother's breast". Being such a crucial experience that no alternative notion would be entertained without provoking a full and violent response.

The modern population has changed. It is not so much the need for identities to engage in political action, but rather the mode of political action itself. Before this, absoluteness was so fully personified that violence was not merely political—it was reality itself. With maturity, political action has become a conceptual form of violence that satisfies the need for relevance in identities without requiring the full expression of absoluteness. Identities now avoid complete absoluteness in order to embrace a reality that transcends their own perception, yet they still fulfill their need for relevance through political expression, one which matters to those in the central community. When society loses regard for political activity, the old adages of violence resurface—though few remain concerned, as the political stage has diminished and thus the window to reality.

A mode of operation that secures the philosophy despite its setbacks is the maintenance of a relationship with the never-ending expanse. Even if the expanse remains abstract, it can dominate one's psyche as a source of connection. This never-ending expanse stems from the notion of an unlimited reality—a concept that can itself become politicized. The challenge in relating to the unlimited expanse is that it transcends any conventional form of relatability. Therefore, to relate to the expanse, one must adopt a vantage point at the furthest edge of one's expansion—though still short of true unlimitedness. This dynamic can give rise to a "super-version" of oneself: a form of selfhood that is both relatable and simultaneously connected to the unlimited expanse at its most developed version.

Only at this precipice can one be said to be in a relationship with one's unlimited expanse. However, there is a caveat: the unlimited nature is effectively curtailed, as one must promptly depart from that relationship—in other words, one must relate that aspect to other notions of existence. In doing so, a more refined form that accurately portrays the expanse can be achieved; otherwise, the ultimate aspect will diminish, leaving only an expansive version rather than a true unlimited expanse. Furthermore, even as this unlimited nature is politicized and applied to society, a genuine relationship can be realized with only a solitary relatable entity to one's personal basis.

Departing from such a relationship is also antagonistic. If done in an overly abstract or rigid manner, it can disrupt the continuum of relationships. By consciously disregarding relational material, one harms the connection to the entire relational spectrum. Both the object of the relationship and the individual suffer from such deliberate disengagement. This is akin to political officials attempting to weaken ideologies through physical confrontation and fear—actions that do little to diminish the ideas but certainly does justice to weaken the bond between academia and the political establishment, arguably the most crucial relationship of any state. When physical divisions disrupt the bond between material and its relationships, the drive for connection is stifled, effectively fracturing the fabric of life perception.

Conversely, in the absence of new relational material, desired relationships may merge the object with the person. In such cases, external material is absorbed into the subconscious, with the components of the relationship merging = indistinguishably.

Some may view this philosophy as myopic for neglecting apparent vulnerabilities, yet it is far more elaborate. This becomes evident when a bitter end is experienced—such as in a significant tragedy. Upon confronting limitations, individuals respond with modesty; rather than with being overwhelmed; they use the occasion to introspect and reexamine their personal lives. Anger is short-lived, and the response is broad enough that the stark exposure of existentialism is replaced by a more personal turn. This is reflected in that call upon the observer to incorporate the experience into their personal development.

Such formulations cannot directly target the enemy— explicit labeling only adds to the complexity. In fact, there may even be a reluctance to label the enemy (and, by extension, the vulnerability) because doing so does not further the notion of the unlimited expanse. Any tension that arises is eventually redirected so that it is not seen as an enduring limitation.

Thus, a primary function of the central community is to offer a sense of expansion—a never-ending journey toward an ultimate end. This is evident when an official asserts that their duty is to reality itself, rather than merely to the society or organization that appointed them. If the central community is indeed a never-ending expanse, then every official associated with it must feel an obligation to that expanse. By assuming a role solely for society, their duties become confined to a narrow institution or conceptual framework.

When an official is merely a "paid worker," they inherently oppose expansive ideas and become bound to simplistic social constructs. Although such officials exist, they are the exception and rarely gain significant prestige or career advancement. When approached about their role as arbitrators of reality, officials often respond with unease. Even expressing cynicism about their role can lead to unseemly communication. Their attachment to this role mirrors that of the populace, which embraces these ideas. When a constituent challenges this announcement from a different standpoint, it results in opposition to the *majority* that the official represents.

A narrative within economic discourse may posits individual aspiration as the primary determinant of socioeconomic mobility. This is another manifestation of expansiveness, suggesting that each individual can access any corner of the economic market and succeed. First, it presupposes that every individual possesses the fortitude and aptitude to achieve such amicability. Second, it assumes that the environment is structured in such a way that one can navigate it effectively. If an environment of distinctive persons is indeed never-ending, every personal interaction should reflect that quality. The principle of expansiveness must extend to individuals themselves; accordingly, an expansive individual is most capable of fully actualizing their expansiveness within a correspondingly expansive environment.

No limitations are observed from any vantage point—neither in the individual nor in the environment. When one retains such a viewpoint and encounters limitations, it is assumed they lack a certain fortitude. However, this limitation is not inherent to the general character but rather a flaw in their understanding. They remain part of the never-ending expanse; the flaw a pretense arising from interactions beyond their control. In fact, this very flaw can provide the courage to move further toward greater expansiveness. Once every limitation is perceived as just another gate toward a final aim, it ceases to be a limitation. Thus, a person can remain part of the never-ending expanse despite seemingly insurmountable obstacles, since these are only quantities of an external structure whose aim is expansion.

Even when highly developed determination exists and the environment appears accountable, we tend to attribute fault to the external structure. Something within that structure remains misunderstood, leading us to assume that the environment is flawed. Recognizing a limitation in the environment's economic structure would render the entire system limited. We cannot simply choose another direction—as might be possible in collective suffering—because the individual has already been tested in both fortitude and aptitude. Thus, this philosophy would never deem the environment faulty in an economic situation where the individual has exerted every ounce of effort.

If one accepts that fortitude is essential to this philosophy, then in any scenario—whether in warfare, diplomacy, or domesticative dynamics—little aggression is displayed given the opposing dynamics. Fortitude is a stance toward an aim, and when that aim is threatened, a measured amount of aggression is natural. However, such fortitude is demanded only in certain arenas, demonstrating that these series of philosophies is not solely about courage. We find fortitude in economic standards emerging from the rejection of limitations, and similarly in athletics. Even when considering economic orientations, an aspect of athletic culture transcends them. Winning is the objective, achieved through fortitude—a quality highly prized. When there is no way to manipulate either the individual or the environment surrounding an objective, fortitude becomes the chosen path. The limitations of a competition are so clearly defined that they cannot be reconfigured to resemble an expansive universe; hence, fortitude remains the only route to victory.

Thus, one may question why a populace adhering to this philosophy gravitates toward entertainment, one specially situating them in a non-expansive universe. The answer lies in their perspective upon entertainment—cherished for those moments when limitations are seemingly broken, evoking the sentiment of a never-ending expanse. This contrasts with other worldviews that value entertainment not for the transgression of limitations but for displays of skill, the expression of identity, and appeal.

The Nature of Intimacy in Philosophy and Culture

Intimacy is the weakness of the practical application of philosophy, and it is difficult to find localities of intimacy within its borders. To clarify the notion of intimacy, it is a locality highly interactive with the psyche, containing informational material at every turn, and is thus considered a poetic encounter. Domestication is the chief example of intimacy; no matter the deviation from that setting, it will still keep one alert to the memorable information instilled upon the psyche. The depth of reception in domestication domain provides enough layered experience to affect the entirety of a person's life. The location of a domestication is a home, and this is the offshoot of that very interactive setting, imparting doses of relevant informational material to the psyche with a simple encounter.

The centric locale, due to its lack of intimacy, relies on sub-identities to provide those provisions. However, even if we were to partake in one of those with all its offerings, we would still lack the intimate locality needed to represent the global aspect of the centric locale. Since the sub-identity is rooted in its preconceived notions of reality—even as it filters in the informational material of the universal culture—it subverts that accounting according to its disposition. Furthermore, it naturally maintains both distance and distaste toward the universal mechanism of society, remaining at odds with its agenda.

Let us consider a communal space as a locality of intimacy offered to the universal experience of the centric locale. This locality represents cultural expressions, which serve as a form of art to experience intimacy in the context of performance. While art forms, especially those demanding communal experiences and dramatic informational material, are always a sound way to create intimacy in a given setting, this aspect is difficult to come by. The continuous need to appeal to an audience demands that the most creative minds impute ingenuity into the program, thereby allowing only a very small number of these spaces to offer this form of intimacy in a large population.

We acknowledge this by the economic dividends that the art forms provide to everyone involved. They are praised in such high regard by the community that they are priced at an exorbitant rate, even though they provide a non-essential part to the population. It is this recognition that proves they are one of the few access points to a form of intimacy. Even though intimacy should not be commodified, in the centric locale—which lacks it more than anything—it becomes a valued item of exchange.

In fact, the entire potency of society relies on these localities of intimacy; without them, even as a prolific entity, it would not be able to interact effectively. Moreover, it would not be able to disseminate its prolific sense through any medium, for it cannot demonstrate itself in a universal sense—akin to a teacher who must explain informational material to a new student through a distilled and intimate method. Had the teacher attempted to convey the material as it is experienced by the psyche, it would be lost on the student. It is no coincidence that many cultural hubs have ascended alongside the expansion of the centric locale as the ruling power of the world. We may credit those mediums with taking things too far, yet we must recognize that the centric locale, in its universal sense, is the entity that expanded itself.

Therefore, what emerges is that creativity is extracted from the entire population to provide for these cultural spaces. There is a cost for that extraction in that it leaves the rest of the population with pseudo-creative individuals to deal with every other aspect of society's happenings. Cultural hubs house most of the creativity, while the rest includes those who could or would not make it to these distinct locations. A town or city that lacks creativity or the willingness to foster it would not be able to replicate these localities of intimacy and would be lost without non-identity intimate provisions.

Cities become interactive localities by being part of these intimate spaces, while anything beyond that—which constitutes the majority of the population—lacks an interactive structure. They may attempt a form of intimacy by pledging allegiance to a sense of belonging; however, that does not create a truly intimate atmosphere. It might be justifiable to say that a grouping of a shared identity would move toward immediate intimacy, but this is not the case for a collective identity, as it will never provide an intimate locality for the universal experience of society. I am always reminded of the imagery of certain individuals who believed themselves intimately attached to a cultural experience and forced themselves into the finest establishments, assuming they had formed and were to partake in their collective way. In the immediate instance that they brought their collective sense to these locations, the cultured and intimate setting was lost, and whatever was enjoyed became the last remnant of a decorated past—with the staff feeling immediate contempt for their presence. Contempt does not breed intimacy.

Collective identity will not work for intimacy, as the universal experience expands past the demarcated perimeter of identity and incorporates every noteworthy interaction and detail within society. Moreover, for a locality to be intimate, it must be separate from the notion of the collective because it needs distinct parameters to provide an almost extraterrestrial setting. It needs to operate as a pseudo-identity, as artistic communities often identify themselves. By preaching the collective sense, it does not allow for a separate encounter with a setting that would then filter the informational material of the universal experience. Similar to a partner who takes the forefront of a relationship, one would be unable to partake in its intimate aspect. Taking account of the entire structure does not allow for the specificity with which intimacy is experienced. The performance is separate in that it is part of an industry, identity, and personnel who provide the experience; however, during the interaction, we experience a form of intimacy with the global experience filtered in from the creators and performers. The moment the collective sense enters the picture, it removes the mystique and demands a wholeness in which no intimacy can reside.

Abstraction in the form of utilizing a conceptualization through multiple domains is a part of philosophy. There is no differentiation in the responses of an interaction, as the objective is paramount—almost to the point of sacredness. This is another manifestation of the non-limited perspective of philosophy, which has no concern with real-time limitations in its purview. In this context, occupation takes on the role of all personhood, with no demarcation apart from that persona. The work objective must be completed despite its interactions with limitations or moral questions.

To illustrate, consider a case in point: a paramedic at the scene of a brutalized victim refused to give a tissue on the grounds that the person refused official treatment. They were not allowed to provide any items or assistance without an official case, so a simple tissue was withheld.

The paramedic identified with the occupation so strongly that there was no inclination to remove that cloak and personify an experience beyond it. They adhered cleverly to the code of rules required by their work, using those rules solely to maintain their occupational identity in its entirety. Thus, they felt the need to explain that their rules did not allow them to provide assistance. This reflects their reluctance to depart from their occupational persona on that occasion, and the rules granted them the right to make that declaration.

We would find a difference if the victim were their relative; in such a case, those rules would not be strictly applied, as the paramedic might be willing to depart from their persona for the situation. Moreover, performing the task of providing a tissue would pose only a very slight risk to their occupation by not adhering fully to the rulebook. Even if we can envision repercussions for both the institution and the paramedic, the risk allows for a humanistic aspect to their work and the rationality to perform actions that align with their personal morality. They are not truly interested in the performance of the rulebook per se, but rather in upholding the complete persona of the occupation. They are assumed to be in complete continuity by following the rulebook, as there is no other measure to prove their allegiance to it. This may be compounded by the fact that the entire organization thinks along the same lines, leading to the assumption that the rule-bearing, defensive approach represents their complete identity.

Even so, there is an understanding that they are not truly interested in the occupation as a purposeful endeavor, but rather in performing the expected identity of it. This expectation represents the bare minimum needed to avoid interaction between occupation and personhood, with a clear rulebook in mind that minimizes human involvement. They do not want to provide the tissue because doing so would require human involvement in their occupation, which would diminish their complete identification with it.

In some respects, there is a certain animosity toward the victim for being the individual whose presence allows them to withhold treatment, even for something as trivial as a tissue. This individual represents the workload, which is inherently humanistic, being the only real patient in need of medical assistance throughout the entirety of their career. As soon as the occasion arises that requires them to perform their task according to the rulebook, the patient becomes part of the occupation and its procedural performance. In this case, the person is outside the perimeter of the occupation and becomes a possible patient that invokes their humanistic sense. This is met with animosity, as providing a tissue that would barely risk their job is deemed too much. It is not that there is a lack of compassion among the populace, but rather that the occupation takes such a significant part of one's persona, often overshadowing the humanistic concerns that accompany it.

Another case to demonstrate this is an organization that acts solely for its organized aspect, having lost its objective or purpose. The only reason it can remain organized is that it is bound by economic security for all participants. The performance of tasks is only to ensure that economic provision continues onward and filters into each participant. There may be a slight objective—namely, that they must have a product or service to exchange in the free market—but this is not the important matter of the structure. At some point, the service may be coerced or assumed, while the product may degenerate or be mislabeled, and this would not be a concern. The organization acts solely as the engine of a machine, in continuous motion. When the economic factors fail, it will crumble without anyone feeling the effects, as they will have already moved on to another empty organization.

This type of structure is rampant under such a philosophy, as the occupation within the organization is personified with the wholeness of personhood, allowing the engine to run smoothly. The humanistic side—the purpose or objective —is not part of their daily movements; instead, movement alone, guided by economic reminders, is the pathway forward. When the objective appears seemingly immoral, a catchphrase of philosophy may arise to suppress any guilt that surfaces.

Thus, the occupation becomes unified with personhood so that a system can operate without limits. Ironically, the individual becomes noticeably limited by adhering to the occupation, being bound to its movements instead of their own. However, the trade-off is willingly accepted so that the person may feel a sense of non-limitation, even as they become a product of serious limitations. There is no alternative for them; if they retain their individualistic sense within the occupation, they do not gain the sense of belonging from it. Additionally, their individualism is compromised by even a simple attachment to a system that does not utilize every aspect of them and surely does not have their expression mapped out onto the organization's floor. Ultimately, everyone seeks a complete experience of non-limitation wherever it may be found.

We find that the sentiment in organizations is that their processes are part of the entirety of the centric locale. Even if they are a pseudo-industry, there is a sense of grandeur in their continuity with the bigger picture. If not, then the organization will find itself limited and unable to offer its participants that sense of belonging. The economic aspect is particularly relevant in this process, as it is part of the free exchange market and is thus attached to everything. The declining organization that focuses solely on economic gains is not doing so solely for the sake of profit, but to produce the effect of being attached to the entirety of the system. Even if they do this in suboptimal ways, they are still assumed to be part of the picture; the economic data supports this assumption.

The Universal Center – Consciousness and Biology

At the center of universal consciousness dissemination, this entity behaves in a peculiar manner. Due to the nature of its energy, it cannot translate into a biological singularity and is marked by colossal oversight. Critics argue that this trait makes it appear as a facade of a genuine center—suggesting that a more developed center would not exhibit such vulnerabilities. They typically fail to offer an alternative center against which their ideals might be challenged. This paradox of consciousness reveals that the most central locale is also the most removed from biological reception.

This is why the center demonstrates its uniqueness only through specific reflective offerings. When it attempts to stake a claim in more biological aspects, it devolves into a parody of itself. For example, clothing—a material element that is not fundamentally biological yet maintains a defined relationship to it—may lose its significance within a universal center. However, when clothing is imbued with a higher level of consciousness, the biological distance is offset. In response to the conscious needs of the moment, the locale that produces appropriate clothing measures is one that remains detached from the center while still interacting competently with it.

Undoubtedly, a more biological element, such as substance, will decline in the universal center, becoming rough on the palate as it attempts to savor something so detached from biological forces. Yet every individual remains bound to their biological center and requires a sense of that connection—even in the most universal locales. When there is an overemphasis on biology, however, the biological input needed during interactions with the universal element is minimized.

The measurement of biological compactness and expansiveness can be understood in terms of necessity. When necessity is great, the biological emphasis is minimal; for instance, if one must relieve oneself, that urgent need diminishes the importance of other biological aspects in the environment. As the body's immediate requirements ease, the environment assumes a relatively greater role. Similarly, sustenance is measured by its necessity—when it is critically needed, the specific contents and the context become secondary.

A universal center, therefore, demands only a minimal degree of biological attention to foster proper interaction. This might manifest as sustenance that is non-essential within the metabolic structure but still offers a hint of sweetness or bitterness. Such elements interact on a biological level without being central to core metabolic needs. Similarly, artistic presentations—which, though not biological necessities, portray elements of biological relation—lose their significance if they fail to connect to a biological element. For instance, abstract art expresses personhood and the mental experience of our system; yet its weak relation to biology means it lacks the vitality found in other artistic expressions.

The extent of biological emphasis is dictated by the necessity of the moment. In times of low necessity, the biological element is expanded; when necessity is high, it is minimized. However, at the universal center—where conscious material emanates at an accelerated rate—the biological component must always remain minimal. The question then becomes: how small? In some cases, even a mere aroma will suffice; in others, a metabolic ingestion might be required. We can never fully depart from the need for biological interaction. Even as conscious material flows faster than we can fathom, we remain bound to our biological centers, though this connection takes on a ceremonial form rather than constituting a major focus.

Another point to consider is the disintegration of beauty and splendor at the center of universality. The closer one approaches the center, the more its inaccessibility becomes apparent—its innate nature being ambiguous. This is comparable to sexuality, where a focus merely on procreation and bodily interaction can dilute its vitality and dynamism. Proximity creates a situation in which the essence cannot fully manifest through further interactions. Much like poetic prose, which assembles a vocabulary that obscures the objective, the final product diverges from its original aim. Although the prose may ostensibly reach the objective, much like the punchline of a joke, it loses the depth of sentimental value or, in the case of humor, its sensibility.

We easily grasp these final objectives—whether it be the punchline of a joke, the sentimental value of a prose piece, or the center of universality—without the need for further dissemination of their inherent value.

What is necessary, however, is the "download" of the objective: its dissemination pending every fissure of the psyche is engaged. For example, when approaching the objective within sexuality without diverse representations to guide us, we may achieve it in time but lack a persona to bring the interaction to life. To embody a complete persona—accounting for every facet of the psyche—there must be relatability across all diverse modes of interaction.

Consider, for instance, a simple prose phrase: "The crisp of Fall." The intent is to evoke the sentimental nature of the fall season. In doing so, the details might refer to the onset of cold that intermingles with hints of warmth, culminating in a sensation described as "crisp." Yet this is not the sole objective. The term "crisp" also denotes a state of food texture—perhaps reminiscent of a slightly overcooked state—and it pertains to the seasonal transition from summer to winter. These represent at least three distinct objectives, not to mention the sub-objectives that lead to them.

Rather than stating "Fall is crisp," we approach it from the perspective of "crisp," as if crispness itself brings about Fall, rather than simply characterizing it. In this way, the universal element of "crisp" interacts with the attributes of Fall, remaining ambiguous as to whether we are addressing the season or the concept of crispness. Typically, we balance the attribute of Fall with a counter-statement, ensuring the prose retains a deliberate ambiguity regarding its objective. Thus, every element of the psyche associated with "crisp" becomes relatable—be it the transition, food texture, cooking temperatures, the waning of Summer, or the onset of Winter. In navigating these multiple objectives, we approach a final, ultimate objective that remains inherently ambiguous. The prose loses its effect if it becomes overly ambiguous, resulting in a lack of clear outcome, merely representing an endless abyss.

Consciousness – Physical Realm

The realm that inhabits the primary layer of consciousness is deeply intertwined with physical manifestation. Much like an individual composed of multiple layers of consciousness, the foremost layer continuously expresses itself in the physical realm. For instance, a profound understanding of the sacred depth of child-rearing—from pregnancy onward—may be embedded in this primary layer. Consequently, such understanding is physically expressed; the individual displays an intuition so deep that it appears entirely natural rather than a product of deliberate, conscious development.

For this reason, the primary layers of consciousness are often unavailable for direct discussion or further conceptual interaction. Having already found expression in the external realm, any attempt to disrupt that flow is fruitless, as physicality remains the definitive metric of existence. When the physical realm expresses itself, it diverges from previous conceptual progress. The physical base testifies through natural actions and environmental responses, and to contest it is to dismiss the highest degree of acknowledged existence.

A dilemma arises when a deeply embedded conceptual layer begins to manifest physically. Once it has made this journey, it is no longer available for additional conceptual integration, having allied itself with a realm that neither can nor should be questioned.

Accordingly, one must engage in physical manifestation so that interaction can occur on that basis, thereby paving the way for a more elaborate conceptual layer. For example, regarding the sacredness of children, if one wishes to overlay a higher conceptual layer upon that understanding, the process requires—not discussion—but physical activity in that regard. When physical interaction with children (or related contexts) occurs, an individual with access to a higher conceptual layer can affect that setting. Although it may seem impossible—since those engaging physically would appear to be unavailable for a grander conceptual layer than the one already expressed—there are intervals when one can depart from the current situation and engage with an imaginative realm. This realm permits a conceptual discussion disconnected from the external world, after which one may return to physical activity and apply a higher conceptual layer.

Naturally, conflict will arise when a higher conceptual layer interacts with the external realm, which demands a physical manifestation of its ideas. For example, if a subordinate conceptual layer is "rummaging," the ensuing physical activity will proceed in a direction that either induces the conceptual layer to be discarded or compels it to prove itself as a genuine component of consciousness. An individual might entertain the idea of society being divided into classes, even deprived of physically embodying that notion. In response, the physical actions may begin to reflect class-related sentiments, allowing the psyche to assess whether this conceptual layer should become an integral fabric of the physical realm or remain a transient thought of momentary value.

A similar process applies to the external realm in its interaction with the individual. In certain environments, the external realm actively seeks the physical manifestation of an individual's mental state. For instance, in work settings that involve inherent danger, groups assess each individual for the physical expression of their conceptual layers. This serves two purposes: first, to ensure that the conceptual continuum within the assemblage remains corresponding, and second, to verify that the individual does not harbor a conceptual layer that has not been integrated into the physical realm.

In the first case, an individual might permit a certain idea while concealing another conceptual layer; however, this is acceptable for the group, which requires a continuum at some scale, though not necessarily at every level. In the second case, merely testing the individual is insufficient—one must observe physical actions as proof of integration. This observation constitutes the second step for trust to develop. Under pressure—during moments of existential vulnerability—there is a transfer of conceptual layers, even those previously hidden, all into the physical realm.

The environment that demands a more pronounced physical manifestation of conceptualizations is determined by either the capacity of the consciousness center or the level of existential threat. In the latter case, as previously elaborated, when physical or emotional danger is present, the physical realm becomes the primary and necessary choice (for example, in the case of combatants). Similarly, when engaging with the consciousness center, physicality is required to transfer elements from the conceptual realm into the external one. The conceptual realm lacks a primal physical aspect; therefore, only its highest components are granted the opportunity to physically manifest in their true form.

The Paradox of Reflection and Existence

There is a reflective perspective that discounts the essential nature of anything, yet it plays a significant role in facilitating reflection on essential aspects. In this view, the highest form of value lies in elements that are highly adaptable—reflective edges from which an essential value can, or would, be regularly extracted. The reasoning is that if a multitude of reflective edges surrounds an essential aspect, it will serve as an instruction for a sure existence.

The error in this view is that, although reflective material grants access to the essential aspect, it does not secure existence in any evocative way. Instead, existence is volatile, and its only remedy is an abundance of existence itself. Access merely places the individual within existence; it does not provide a pathway to truly interact with or become part of it. In fact, by using so much reflective material, one becomes distracted from engaging in the very dealings that follow such access.

A common outcome is that gaining access becomes the sole objective, accompanied by a façade of humility in never having contained the genuine point within that essential realm. This is not true humility—the intended objective is to remain distracted by the act of obtaining, thereby avoiding the complex and intricate process of managing that level of access. What becomes evident is that most interactions involve external material that theoretically grants access to the essential nature through its reflective properties, but in practice, serves only to distract one from entering into that essential access. It is almost as if the essential access is itself a piece of reflective material, rendering it unnecessary to ever depart from the mode of reflection, since the essential nature becomes a reflection as well.

However, the logic lacks coherence; if the essential nature is a mere reflection, then it cannot be a genuine essential point. The disjointed reply might be that all of nature is merely a reflection. Yet, this leaves us without logical continuity, asserting that all of nature is a reflection and presupposes an absolute essential point. Otherwise, the entire argument is flawed, since the nature of reflection depends on an assumed absolute essential point.

The manner in which one navigates this logical inconsistency is through the degree of interaction with external stimuli. At one extreme lies the existential dread of failing to interact with a singular reflective point, representing the most dissociated departure from essential reality—given that this reflective point is assumed to be singular. In contrast, the reality is that reflective material comprises infinite points through which one can access essential reality; this perspective takes the cautious assumption that this specific point is the only mode of reflection.

The Illusion of Reflection: Navigating the External and Essential

This approach cannot possibly lead to an experience of reflecting on the essential point, since a pathological focus on one singular aspect carries the paradox of treating it as both essential and merely reflective. One might convince oneself that their interaction is directed toward an essential item; however, upon closer scrutiny, it becomes clear that it is only reflective material.

An individual may assume that a particular point is essential in order to find refuge in a reflective haven. This is analogous to attempting to reside in a house that exists only as a mirror image. Although the house appears in the mirror, it is understood to be merely a reflection rather than the genuine structure. Yet, by avoiding engagement with essential material, the individual justifies the mirrored house as a facet of existence—a claim on reality. Similarly, if the genuine house is itself a reflection of something more, who is to say that the reflective house does not possess its own genuine nature? While we cannot disprove such a claim, we must acknowledge that a healthy interaction between the essential and the reflective is necessary.

It is easy to assert that the material before us is essential while the interaction itself remains merely reflective. For instance, a genuine home is recognized by its surroundings as an essential component. However, often the interaction is purely reflective, and no one claims an essential point within that domain. Instead, the individual stays in a reflective state to avoid confronting the hardships and complexities of essential points. They label the experience as essential solely to avoid deeper reflection—continuing to interact as if it were just a house in a mirror. This situation cannot be dismissed; it represents a warped psyche that is difficult to assess from an external perspective.

Conversely, there is a pathological focus on reflective points. Consider any physical body: although we agree that such a body is not the essential point despite its powerful reflective quality, one might still claim it to be essential. In doing so, the individual clings to the body to avoid confronting the internal realm within it. The purpose here is not to engage with the reflective material that points toward an essential truth, but rather to avoid that truth by overstimulating the reflective aspect until it becomes the sole reality. This approach offers a sense of existence, albeit from the outermost point on the essential spectrum—even though any reflective material inherently mirrors many essential points.

The problem with finding refuge at the reflective edge is that it demands a justification for its importance relative to the apparent essential aspects. Because society does not agree that such reflective material constitutes essential nature, one is forced to adopt a cautious intellectual framework that connects a pathological focus on the reflective to an essential realm. This connection is often established through relationships, which serve as a powerful mechanism to bind disparate aspects of nature—even in the absence of a strict logical system.

For example, an individual might claim that detaching from that reflective material results in a loss of relationship, implying that the reflective is the habitat for social interaction. In this scenario, reflective material becomes the medium for grandiose relationships, much like an environment that nurtures romance.

Because of its significance in relationships, one may choose to remain within that reflective domain to foster further connections. This argument, however, can be countered by noting that relationships are supported by the environment—in fact, by any environment —and not solely by the reflective edge. Moreover, the process of evolution has selected reflective material as a habitat where one can remain attached and then seek relationships to justify that pathological focus. These relationships are not pursued for their own sake but rather as tools to maintain a chosen position.

Even in the absence of an existing relationship, when reflective material is questioned, the individual may seek any form of relationship in order to remain exactly where they are. They do not aim to gain or actively engage in these new relationships; sometimes, they may even approach them with contempt or hatred. A positive relationship is not necessary— merely any relationship will suffice to avoid venturing beyond the reflective material.

When interactions are approached in a way that would normally stimulate genuine existential movement, the individual instead demands the impossible in order to remain in a state of discontent within the relationship. This demand allows them to remain existentially attached to the relationship—a bond nurtured solely to justify their pathological refuge in a reflective domain.

Such a stance creates an impossible interaction. The individual refuses to engage with the reflective material of that domain—which contains essential aspects—and also avoids interacting with the reflective base itself, as that would require genuine self-reflection. Furthermore, they reject engaging with the relationship that was constructed merely to justify their reflective refuge. Any attempt to produce a genuine effect or authentic existential interaction is thwarted because the entire relationship exists solely to support a particular pathological position.

Yet, as with all relationships, this approach creates vulnerability. High demands are imposed—demands that are theoretically attainable —so that the individual may then engage existentially. However, there is no guarantee that the other person or society will meet these demands, leaving the relationship in a state of deadlock.

The more deeply an individual or society embeds itself in the reflective edge —devoid of essential engagement—the more interactions focus on the intricate details of that reflective layer. Discussions are treated as if they are of utmost importance, detailing the specifics of some external reflective material. These details are complex and intricate, intended to compensate for the nature of the essential points. Methods of engaging with essential aspects are employed during interactions with the reflective, creating the appearance of existential movement and progress—a through line for ordinary conversation.

The final outcome of these conversations is a clearer understanding of the singular reflective edge, which ultimately produces no real societal or individual effect. The only genuine result is a more unified stance on remaining in the same place, achieved by applying intellectual jargon to validate its relevance.

In fact, conversations are pursued with great intensity to produce a stimulating effect that compensates for the lack of genuine existential interaction with essential material. Hours may pass in discussion, creating a sense of stimulation that could otherwise be achieved in a single moment of truly related dialogue. The details become more captivating because generalities compel one to reach beyond the reflective material; even the shade or color of that reflective layer becomes the most important aspect, despite having no inherent existential purpose.

This tendency is also observable in monetary dealings, which naturally serve as a reflective edge. Monetary transactions pertain only to human relationships and labor, reflecting these interactions without providing a domain from which many essential aspects can be derived. When one enters the realm of monetary dealings, there is a compulsion to avoid the genuine reflective material that seeks the essential aspects—by claiming that the field is abstract and complex, the psyche is convinced that these dealings are intentionally essential.

Furthermore, the high value placed on abstraction produces a general framework for contextual interaction. When something is universalized—for example, discussing "the child" rather than personal anecdotes—we transform that child into a universal concept that resonates with anyone who understands childhood or outcomes in general. Thus, generating an abstract framework can be a sure way to claim that something is essentially important.

However, the individual's psyche will not fully engage with that framework; if it did, the specific abstraction would lose its relevance for its own sake, becoming merely a tool for another perspective. In the case of "the child," if we remain fixated on the description—even if those interacting with the material may benefit existentially—we risk being scrutinized for using a specific point to gain from a universal concept when the universal realm is far more expansive than "the child."

A similar pattern is observable in monetary dealings, which may be universalized to make an existential claim even though those involved may not gain much from it. If they did, as with all universal aspects, they would shift fleetingly from one point to another without anchoring in any reference for long.

It can generally be agreed that monetary dealings are deeply connected to the essential and can be considered as such. Most individuals compelled to engage in monetary transactions do so because they are seeking an underlying essential point. Although they do not pursue further production of that point, they use the reflective edge of monetary dealings both to sustain the relationship without progressing it and to find refuge from the relationship through this potent reflective barrier.

Thus, monetary dealings serve both to avoid the deeper relationship and to remain attached to it, appearing irrelevant as an essential point within that relationship. In this scenario, monetary dealings remain existentially affixed while still playing a role in the overall mode of existence. Generally, remaining existentially affixed would render one irrelevant to the psyche; therefore, to compensate for such choices, a specific point is required—one that is not existentially related yet is sufficient to generate the assumption of one's own relevance as an element of existence.

Alcohol and the Rearrangement of the Psyche

Alcohol is a defining characteristic for the formulation and the disturbance of this philosophy. Its effects direct cognition toward avenues not readily pursued and rearrange the psyche with the aim of producing sensational change and insightful deliverance. This state can be overused under the thesis which asserts the status quo as perfected. Alcohol rejects such a perspective outright and places the psyche—not in a mere vacuum of replacement but in its truest form—albeit within a rearranged system where dormant motivations are assumed to be mastered, while those that sustain daily control are neglected.

The Altered Reality of the Inebriated Individual

The inebriated individual directly experiences a reality different from the one assumed, both in self-perception and in the social sphere. Observing an inebriated person reveals a contesting reality that could prove effective in broader society when applied by a competent individual. Thus, inebriated individuals may cross normal social boundaries, displaying a latent social motivation for more obtrusive and deliberate connections with strangers. This may not be the case in every culture, where the innate motivation for isolation is more prevalent due to the natural setting of hyper-social activity. For example, one might imagine a party scene where higher connection is sought; yet in a typical social setting, a more unsatisfactory distance is maintained. When that distance is mitigated, the scene loses its effect, as the dormant motivation has been addressed.

The main point is that a rearrangement of the psyche produces a genuine motivation which reveals societal dormancy and alternative realities. This is not conducive for a culture that presumes its reality to be all-encompassing. Those who adhere excessively to the effects of a rearranged psyche may be found in surplus within such a culture. The very opposition of the social environment toward a changed psyche drives individuals to seek further rearrangements that may better suit society. However, this proves futile, as no agreement on any other reality can be reached; the only effective process to access that sentiment of "fun" is to fulfill the requirements of the psyche despite social opposition. The notion of "fun" serves merely as a metaphor for a productive psyche that accesses dormant motivations despite social pressure.

Substance, Interactivity, and the Psyche

Everything appears proper under the influence of a substance in locales distinguished from the central locality by political and geographical separation. Because these locales, by definition, engage interactively with the center, the substance affects the brain only within the realm of interactivity. One of the great benefits of the mind's components that deal with interactivity is that they validate themselves through a cyclical process—new information merely propagates its current state. To understand psychic interactivity, we must attend to external interactions, where group dynamics mirror each other with slight nuances and deviations among proponents. Essentially, interactivity within a group validates individual content in much the same way as interactive processes within the psyche.

Substance can guide interactivity to different arenas and regions, allowing one to participate in a mental sociality that has not previously been enabled. Although interactivity can be entertained without substance, the substance exerts an immediate and controlled effect by directing interactivity in a novel direction. This is why substance regularly participates in sociality; it essentially mirrors the same function. Individual regulation of substance follows a similar order, allowing internal sociality to emerge—and even encouraging self-dialogue to engineer a more pertinent social experience.

The Effects of Substance in Different Localities

When substance is consumed in an interactive locale that is politically and geographically separate (especially by sea), its effect favors a certain form of interactivity. Every psychic exposure in these localities is founded on interactivity; thus, there is little risk of substance taking effect outside that setting.

However, within the central locality and its structural influence—defined by connected land and the transportation of sociality—substance is more likely to extend beyond the interactive realm. This leads to the realm of consciousness which, under the influence of substance, can carry the psyche into novel or existential territories far superior in regulating its movement. Unlike the interactive realm, the consciousness realm does not mirror itself; rather, it reflects nature and all that is possible in existence. This opens the psyche to a new structural reality which, under the influence of substance, may lead to areas that are existentially destructive to both the psyche and sociality.

The Psyche's Vulnerability to Consciousness and Substance

No longer is the substance safeguarded by interactivity; instead, the psyche is exposed to all possibilities that substance might introduce—a direction that may not be controlled or even desired by either the psyche or sociality. This presents a significant problem, potentially leading to substance abuse. Once there is regulation of consciousness and its particular structure, the individual will want to continue that process, even if it involves doses of consciousness that the otherwise wholesome psyche or sociality would not endorse.

This situation is comparable to joining a cult, where the psyche enters a realm with a newfound reality structure afforded by the substance and seeks to regain that effect repeatedly. During sober stages, the psyche struggles to achieve the same degree of consciousness because the dosage obtained during substance use is nuanced and does not integrate well with sober sociality. To recapture that lost consciousness—absent during sober intervals because it is characteristically opposed—one must continue using the substance, as there appears to be no alternative. As with a cult, the longer the influence is maintained, the more challenging it becomes to separate, with little possibility of reintegrating into normal conscious sociality. Normal consciousness operates on a different level, necessitating even a minimal effect of consciousness rather than none.

The Struggle between Consciousness and the Central Locality

Under the rubric of the central locality, consciousness is perceived as a life form and, devoid of its substance, is experienced as a psychic death that can lead to suicidal tendencies. Genuine consciousness proves its reality and relevance by taking the place of organic life. A lack of consciousness does not restore one to a pastoral existence, as the psyche recognizes the exposure hovering above. By merely acknowledging this, one may find themselves in an existence that feels organically alive yet conceptually lost in the realm of consciousness, as if existence itself were null. We might perceive this consciousness as an agent operating within the central locality, dispelling its regulation among all conscious individuals by declaring, "Life form is based on this criterion, and those who disagree will experience a lifeless form." The psyche concurs with this establishment, for consciousness is akin to a life form—even if it possesses an organic substrate separate from its exposure.

The individual under this establishment faces an impossible choice: to ignore the exposure is to either embrace a cult-like dosage of that consciousness or to experience a lack of life form. One might attempt to provide a pastoral and organic function to gain a semblance of life, but the deficiency remains, leading to existential disarray without a solution. A small amount of substance may automatically direct one toward a conscious attachment, allowing entry into that haven with no departure. Yet departure would mean regressing into the oblivion of a lifeless form—a form of death for the psyche— leaving only slight exposure to consciousness through the substance. As the substance fails to direct proper social function, it eventually becomes more cult-like, causing the individual to become increasingly confined, with a diminishing ability to escape.

The Betrayal of Sociality and the Individual Psyche

There is a betrayal of sociality from substance influence under the rubric of this central locality. Sociality is recognized not as an interactive body (as most presume) but as a collection of proponents representing themselves to engineer an exposure of consciousness. When discussing sociality within the central locality, we refer to each member as part of a system that follows a conscious sentiment, where every interaction contributes to that representation. There is no interactivity solely to validate individuals and groups; rather, interactivity serves to further that consciousness in its many forms, creating vulnerability gaps mentioned in other chapters. Genuine interactivity is betrayed when individuals or groups fail to participate with sufficient validation—either by being less interactive or, worse, by de-validating that interactivity. The psyche follows the same pattern: self-betrayal occurs when one does not allow its differing parts to interact and validate one another, instead segregating distinguished components despite their relevance to the whole.

Under the consciousness center, betrayal occurs when one fails to properly represent the collective conscious awareness. There is no betrayal in the lack of interactivity; in fact, it is praised when one does not seek external validation but participates in following the sentiment of that consciousness. Once betrayal occurs, the individual is considered psychotic— for how could someone disengage from conscious awareness unless their psyche degenerates. This is entirely accurate;

disengagement from conscious subjection is impossible if the psyche functions normally. Even children, despite their high degree of interactivity, engage with that exposure to the extent that their psyche permits consciousness. A child, under this rubric, is primarily an interactive composition, yet the available components for consciousness engage without their control or regulation.

This underscores the importance of shielding the child from excessive conscious exposure under this influence by providing a firm educational and contextual foundation. Even the aspects of their psyche that are accessible to consciousness must be filtered through a robust context and identity. When one employs a contextual layer to regulate conscious exposure, they are not disengaging but rather choosing to engage from a vantage point that is less existential and more informational. There may be an attempt to disengage from consciousness altogether by imposing such a strong contextual overlay that no light can penetrate inwardly. However, this would eventually lead the psyche into dysfunction, as contextual regulation of this depth would be overcome by exposure.

Context is a double-edged sword: while it regulates the degree of exposure, it does not control the depth. Thus, what manages to penetrate the other side can be highly volatile and existentially stimulating. This is why individuals emerging from long-term trauma environments become most troubled upon departure. They have acquired a potent contextual base within those confines, which shields them from irrelevant external exposures; however, once they leave, that same contextual lens destabilizes their perception of the external realm. Although this lens provides a sophisticated vantage point, certain exposures will inevitably penetrate that lens. Because the contextual layer is so effective at avoiding exposure, what does make entry will existentially destabilize the individual, becoming unsettling for the psyche. Furthermore, as the contextual layer has regulated the psyche, there is no ability to handle what breaches that sphere, causing existential destabilization.

Therefore, while contextualization can effectively prevent unwanted exposure in stable environments, it can be detrimental if significant exposure does occur. For example, in a cult environment, members might be shielded from conscious exposure; yet when exposure does occur, it becomes traumatic and taboo for the group—existentially uprooting them without the tools to process the experience.

Perception, Consciousness, and Social Boundaries

Alcohol holds a promise it cannot fulfill; it appears capable of delivering an interaction but ultimately misses its expectation. It is used as an interactive substance with the central locality and its conscious subjection, serving as an aide to consciousness. Ideally, a substance of value would be the central theme, and simple biological amenities might suffice— if not for the restructuring of the systematic position necessary to distinguish true interaction. The ability of a substance to alter the state of consciousness does not inherently require remedy; only when there is biological necessity or ritualistic engagement can any regular activity serve as an interactive mediator between oneself and consciousness. Alcohol makes its promise through its external manifestation, so that one does not have to proceed through a complex process to achieve interaction.

Biological necessity—as noted in other works—occurs when one reaches a level of experiential need, the fulfillment of which becomes optimized by including a conceptual arrangement that provides nuance for conscious interaction. The ritualized aspect involves providing a conceptual parameter for interaction through various biological needs, creating a habitat that fosters prioritized engagement with consciousness. History shows that certain substances—chief among them alcohol—have served as mediators without the need to endure biological necessity or ritualistic arrangement. In fact, ritualized arrangement often coincides with alcohol because both perform similar processes: one internally and the other externally. We can perceive an evolution where there is a gradual shift from an external mechanism to an internal one, in which alcohol becomes the nemesis of the central locality and its conscious subjection.

The provision of an external mechanism for interacting with consciousness appears to regulate proper social decorum. However, the individual psyche does not truly gain interaction from alcohol use, because alcohol immediately alters consciousness, converting the psyche into an interactive domain.

With interactivity embodied, direct engagement with consciousness becomes impossible, as the only method of interaction becomes that which is based solely on interactivity. Consequently, the consciousness retrieved through such interaction is completely altered—disfigured, in fact—leaving the individual as a reflection of dysfunction and misinterpreted consciousness. The interaction is indirect; only through disruptive engagement does a formulation emerge from the subjection, which can be drastically troubling to the psyche's processes and its understanding of consciousness. Moreover, even consciousness imprinted in a dysfunctional manner becomes part of the overall continuum, influencing even sober interactions with a trace of dysfunction.

History allowed such a procedure to take effect for two main reasons. First, the repression of an external substance enabled interaction with consciousness through its natural manifestation, ensuring that the process remained a learning experience for others to perform it properly in the regular form. As well, for children and infantile stages of development, for it to be a performance of how to occur in the interaction with consciousness via substance. Without these repressions, infantile stages would not be able to understand the process of interacting with consciousness through any substance. (E.g., adolescent or young adult)

The second reason is that there remains a reciprocation of consciousness through alcohol—even if it is dysfunctional rather than aligned with the intended parameters—and this is preferable to no reception at all. Even in the contemporary era, there are individuals who progress in conscious interaction via alcohol use; they either gain a dysfunctional interpretation or ritualize it. This occurs to such an extent that the entire thought process is based on an interactive boundary regulated by context, which prevents unmediated thought material from entering. This means that the final product of interaction— retrieving certain conscious material—is based on a dysfunctional interpretation, sufficient only to disrupt the contextual parameters.

Thus, alcohol becomes a substance that is significant for the central locality, representing infantile stages or the hope that gaining a measure of dysfunctional consciousness outweighs having no interaction with consciousness. This is why the central locality is particularly focused on requiring some form of ritualistic or contextual parameter: the dysfunctional reception, though flawed, is usually more promising when some context is present. The initial representation is not for the individual but for the group's interaction, helping them to develop both a conceptual and existential understanding of how to interact with consciousness—something that could be achieved through methods that do not require mass alcohol engagement. This is why we will find an ambiguous nature towards alcohol from the center locality because of these aspects, which cannot ignore the substance but also cannot allow its presence.

Identities in the Centric Locale

Intimacy localities are quite extensive, protruding into every corner and offering the best experience of their distinctive sub-state. They seem incapable of imagining any attachment more elaborate than their immediate circumference, assuring us that their vitality is derived from within their very framework. However, despite this impression, these small localities are merely an innate manifestation of the entire state—or more precisely, the dominant contextual influence. They assert that their identity has generated specific sentiments, which can be traced in the tradition's repository.

These sources, serving as proof of the intimate experience, are identified post hoc. Once intimacy permeates the environment, intellectuals promptly examine the database to locate the origin. There is a widespread belief that logic is intrinsic, as sources—once elaborated in a distinctive context—become transparent evidence. Those who adhere to a rational framework find this evidence sufficient. However, we cannot confirm the subtle gap between the initial context of inspiration and those who pursued its origin, since this gap is nearly impossible to pinpoint. A secondary gap emerges in the intense attachment of an individual to the source, which, if recognized, might have revealed the true process. What precisely constitutes their specific attachment to this aspect, and why were these relationships not identified earlier?

Political Dynamics and Intimacy

When individuals act intuitively and honestly, their influence extends beyond the confines of their identity, connecting them to an overarching political entity and its contemporary cultural movements. These relationships, culminating in the final attachment to this aspect, are challenging to trace through any logical continuum. Such attachments may form alike a street sign, manner of speech, or even a change in a store's products. The only certainty is that they ultimately reconnect to the political entity known as the centric locale. Consequently, anyone unwilling to accept this entity will be unable to follow its cultural movements, thereby losing the intimacy inherent in the identity to which they embody. Thus, any identity in conflict with the overarching political entity cannot experience intimacy.

When intimacy occurs, it is due to a subtle attachment—occasionally oriented negatively—that fosters a particular sense within the identity. The greater the conflict between the identity and the political establishment, the more negative the relationship becomes, ensuring that some form of intimacy emerges within their unique sphere. An identity under a political establishment cannot maintain distance without a distinctly charged relationship. The political entity, as the highest order, remains in constant dynamic interplay with its subordinate elements. When an identity chooses to oppose the political entity, it must adopt a negative relationship, as detachment is not an option. Although this negativity appears detrimental in the political realm, in respect to the identity it functions as a form of material information that ultimately enhances their intimacy, becoming positive in its final analysis.

Precisely because the structure of this political entity does not inherently facilitate an intimate experience, these small localities not only acquire intimacy for themselves but also assume the role of its origin. This entitlement is understandable, given the absence of a reasonable alternative. With minimal effort and basic parameters, any identity can manifest a similar intimacy across the state, even when identities differ significantly.

These identities embody the entire interactive influence of the state, as one requires these mediums to engage with it. Lacking a representative interactive structure of their own, they cannot be directly networked with. Any attempt to do so either reinforces nationalism—a fallacy previously discussed—or results in an overload of information that is disconnected from the individual. One might even liken homelessness to this phenomenon: without a locality to engage with the state, there is an overload of information. Such identities can be seen as public personalities saturated with state information, lacking a mechanism to dissect or dilute such information, leading to an inconsistent experience. A transcript of their speech might reveal an entire database of current cultural information, albeit scrambled and incoherent. This content becomes immediately intrusive to because it comprises the most relevant information, compelling one to fully engage with the political entity.

As previously noted, the political entity is a relationship after which one cannot easily extricate oneself. Consequently, individuals will intuitively distance themselves from its current information, as engaging would oblige them to address it—

especially if they have found comfort in previous information that the present material might displace.

The city becomes a habitat for those either ready to move to the next topic or resigned to abandoning autonomous engagement with information. An identity cannot reside at the heart of the city, as it cannot systematically provide intimacy with each new encounter. Instead, it must remain on the periphery to prevent current material from distracting the intimacy associated with an established body of information.

We term this interval between the intimacy of the identity and the current set of cultural information provided by the political entity as "lag time." The duration of this lag correlates with the depth of intimacy: an identity with deep intimacy will have fixed data reaching back to previous decades or even centuries, whereas shallow intimacy corresponds to more recent data.

The question arises: can an identity operate with a data set that is temporally adjacent nevertheless evoke deep intimacy? Generally, this does not appear to be the case. However, on an individual level, is it possible to experience immediate intimacy following the presentation of new material? This would require a process similar to that of the identity itself—executed without impediment. The identity requires this period to process information among its components, naturally repelling incoming data as it integrates previously acquired material.

The identity processes information by establishing parameters and integrating it through biological connections. It internalizes the information, allowing the organismic structure to incorporate the material as if it were part of its very flesh. Naturally, not all material can be seamlessly integrated into our organic structure, although immediate assimilation is sometimes possible. The identity requires a stint to avoid systemic degradation. Similarly, an individual must consider what is applied to their organic structure, as an overload can undermine the system. When this happens, the material is superficially experienced and loses its poetic quality. Overloading an identity with current material diminishes the potency of its conceptual framework, ultimately failing to provide a habitat of intimacy—much like a government institution inundated with political information but incapable of fostering a genuine sense of closeness.

Thus, people are wary of proximity to these localities, as they generate non-intimacy in all their interactions.

Individuals possess mechanisms to cope with excessive intimacy. This mechanism diminishes the entire apparatus, preventing any material from fully integrating into the organism. The organic structure itself reduces its attachment to the psyche, thereby preventing the psyche from imposing these intrusions. Consequently, intimacy can only be achieved intermittently and with select pieces of information. Any further attempts will not only hinder meaningful interaction but also undermine the entire process of intimacy.

Philosophical Underpinnings and Political Realities

While this dynamic is a natural political reality for democratic establishments, the centric locale is distinct in that it has adopted a position that transcends traditional political structures. It aims to supersede any democratic formation, framing the administration of democracy as the realistic embodiment of reality. In this political construct, reality is democratic—not merely a conceptualization of ideas, but a direct adherence to the essence of reality itself. Philosophical inquiries into the centric locale often err by concentrating on overt ideas that, although noteworthy, do not reveal the true nature of the phenomenon.

A careful study of reality reveals that it is democratic in certain respects. When defined loosely as self-derived entities operating in unison, reality cannot be simply characterized as free or equal. Aspects of freedom and equality are evident in any entity's expression—entities that are inherently free to express and receive that expression equally. For instance, when a zebra is killed by a leopard, the zebra's pain is an expression perceived by the environment without prejudice. There are no natural elements that seek to diminish the zebra's pain, nor mechanisms to control its psyche and mitigate that pain. Such attributes are uniquely human and can be deemed anti-nature. According to this thesis, human attributes that distort the observed reality of expression or provide a means to detach it from the psyche are inherently problematic.

This framework allows each entity to follow its path of interest, even though it will inevitably encounter another entity that impedes it: the zebra's instinct to survive conflicts with the leopard's drive for sustenance. Thus, it is not about protecting the zebra's will to live or its ultimate expression, but rather allowing the leopard's natural course to unfold. If we were to halt the leopard, we would be implying that environmental expression is problematic; similarly, if we were to assist the zebra, we would suggest that the environment—and hence reality—is flawed. True freedom entails that both realities operate uninterrupted, so long as the entity's expression is not impeded. When freedom centers on a specific entity's expression, it restricts the broader reality that sustains it. Ultimately, the animals are equal in that their expressions remain absolute, despite any environmental advantages.

If the centric locale seeks to expand or protect a particular expression, it does so to support another entity that actively attempts to diminish it. Yet, the entity that seeks to diminish the additional expression is also part of environmental reality. The core thesis of this philosophy posits that reality is devoid of such attributes. The presence of these attributes is deemed anti-reality, as they represent misguided conceptualizations of reality. This is the sole perspective from which the centric locale offers its opinion: anti-reality conceptualizations from which it originated.

The challenge is that social relationships invariably embody these attributes, which, when exposed, warrant political scrutiny. This is an enduring aspect of human affairs, as we interact with various conceptualizations, human competition revolves around the contentious ideas. The conflict between the leopard and zebra is purely physical, where the one with greater physical prowess prevails. (Arguably with a slight competition in the conception sphere) In contrast, human conflicts predominantly concern competing conceptualizations, where the more dominant ultimately prevails.

Given this, humans can develop a conceptualization that functions solely to deactivate another. This is analogous to currency, which in its conventional role is an exchange of products or services yet can also generate dividends independent of that exchange. This facet of value generation will always exist, as will the capacity to employ conceptualizations to reorder the dynamics of any conflict. In a political establishment, such mechanisms are designed to eliminate these manifestations, functioning according to a conceptualization of anti-conceptualization.

The centric locale cannot question the validity of the conceptualization that reveals its antithetical counterpart, as it does not hold itself accountable for differentiating the two. As long as the conceptualization appears valid, it is accepted without considering that it might represent an alternative form of anti-conceptualization. When the presumed conceptualization is, in fact, its antithesis, it undermines the entire political establishment, rendering its own worst attribute. This would invalidate the philosophy and ultimately lead to the collapse of the political structure.

This vulnerability is expected to be addressed by the judicial body, which can be employed to validate the intentional aspects of any conceptualization through legal interplay. However, the judicial body remains subservient to the political entity, and when the latter falters, so does the former. The only remedy for such vulnerability lies in the self-awareness of those who generate these conceptualizations, or in their willingness to recognize systematic errors in their thinking; ultimately, the responsibility rests upon the individual.

Administering a political establishment strictly by the rules of reality would require a deft sleight of hand. Rather than adhering to the democratic principle of eliminating these two attributes from society—which would position the political entity as the ultimate arbiter of reality and thereby undermine reality itself—the system is designed to remain as flexible as possible. The fundamental thesis of the establishment is reality itself, understood as freedom and equality in the manner previously described. If we reach a point where reality, or our perception of it, changes, then the abstract concepts of freedom and equality can be adjusted accordingly. Since these concepts theoretically apply to any political entity, they serve as the foundation for the written documents and judicial processes underpinning this philosophy. Indeed, we can trace the process of intent back to the original proponents, who sought the removal of these two attributes from the political establishment of their state of origin.

The Domestication in the Center Locality

The Challenge of a Domestication in the Center Locality

The ability to establish a domestication within the center locality is determined by certain parameters. When we use the notion of a domestication, we refer to the most pertinent locality that resembles the interactive body. We encounter a problem from the outset: if a locality seeks to separate and distinguish itself from the external sociality, it may find an outcome that doesn't provide that haven.

Because the exhibition of a center locality is so potent and permeable, any attempt to separate from it in order to provide an interactive experience will yield the opposite result. The exposure will penetrate that isolated space, creating a realm of consciousness that, instead of interacting with all possibilities, is met with a reimagination of a certain dosage of consciousness. Although this may seem like an interactive experience, it is, in fact, a manifestation of siphoned consciousness that does not reconnect with its source.

This type of experience is akin to a cult, which offers a haven of a particular consciousness experience separated from the helm of consciousness. Whatever is gained will come at the expense of the wholeness that must eventually be incorporated. Therefore, any attempt to create a completely interactive locality within the structure of the center locality can be seen as a separation of consciousness.

Nature as a Quintessential Locality

While we have established the inability to have a completely interactive locality within the center due to the high level of exposure, certain interactive properties still exist. The quintessential locality is nature, which these locales have come to know as parks. Nature possesses the quality of being completely aligned with a fundamental reality; regardless of its interaction, it will not be deemed a specific manifestation of consciousness. There is no guiding principle for its locality, so we cannot say that such a park siphons off consciousness in a manner that distinguishes it from the center locality.

This same principle applies to all localities that do not represent a guiding principle beyond that of public space. When we consider a transportation locality, we cannot establish a principle that would cause it to become a separation of consciousness. However, these seemingly interactive localities do not enact a fully interactive experience; instead, they become havens of a consciousness flow that can be experienced.

While these pseudo-interactive localities can manifest an interactive attribute that receives and distributes the consciousness experience, they will not provide an interactive haven that allows for isolationist exposure. Instead, there is a defined direction to the interactivity—a methodology that demands engagement, and only those who follow the consciousness will fully benefit. Others entering the locality with the intention of embracing all forms of interaction may become lost in that direction, absorbing little of the intended information.

This is why these localities are very reliant on present sociality, and during intervals without sociality, the localities take on different properties. Instead of being a receptacle of the consciousness flow, the localities become interactive, as would any interactive locality, but then apply the conjecture of siphoning off a substance of consciousness.

During the night, these localities become terribly inadequate in meeting their regular daily and social functions. During business hours, they contain the previously mentioned interactive ability, but outside of those hours, interaction takes precedence. Any locality that directs its interaction outside the consciousness flow will transform into a form of exposure that does not integrate with the overall conscious subjection.

A domestication, if it attempts to engage beyond a simple locality to receive the consciousness flow, will experience only a partial dose of consciousness. This results in the domestication becoming antithetical to its intended purpose.

Rather than acting as a receptacle of the flow, it becomes a domain that destabilizes the surrounding realm by siphoning off only part of its substance.

Even if the locality appears to be interactive—much like a cult—it is ultimately based on the interaction of a fixed dosage of consciousness. What initially seems like a breath of fresh air turns stale when one realizes that the gained interaction makes their reality structure antithetical to the external realm, further incentivizing isolation.

The validation provided by an interactive locality that delivers a specific dosage of consciousness is wholesome. However, as we are struck by the inability to experience the full consciousness in an interactive manner; we become disassociated from its structure. Maturity, then, allows one to adapt and achieve an interactive experience of the flow through one's own methodology.

This contextual realm serves as both a lens and a housing from which to interact with that flow from a vantage point that permits personal engagement. The personal context compensates for the shortcomings of a structural interactive locality; the problems inherent in the structural setting are less relevant within the psyche.

We notice the difficulty in an interactive locality becoming anything other than a receptacle for the consciousness flow or siphoned consciousness. The former, even as an objective, lacks direction in its receptivity; thus, exposure may be present but not personally interactive. The latter advances only to become destabilized within the entire system. However, the contextual overlay of the psyche does not typically suffer from these problems.

Although the contextual realm can function simply as a container for the flow of consciousness without fostering personal interaction, it also holds a more advanced capacity. This realm can transition into a space that is both highly interactive and personal, thereby enabling exposure to be evocatively engaged. However, a highly contextualized layer might mirror a cult-like environment, where engagement is confined to a fixed measure of consciousness, never allowing for departure from that limited perspective.

A middle ground exists—though it is challenging to create within the structural realm—a space where the contextual layer remains both permeable to the flow of consciousness and interactive on a personal level. Within this spatial framework, the psyche forges an ideal locality that external structures cannot offer.

The contextual realm is prone to rapid shifts into extremes: it can either become overly exposed to the flow of consciousness or provide a deeply personal interaction at the expense of reintegration with the overall consciousness flow. In cases of overexposure, the psyche initially encounters a state of absolute exposure devoid of nuanced distribution; subsequently, this exposure begins to transform into an interactive experience. Given that consciousness is not intrinsically interactive, even an initial exposure—though it may resemble consciousness—becomes detached from personal integration.

Subsequently, the flow of consciousness is reinterpreted as interaction, manifesting an experience of deeply engaged involvement. This transformation poses problems, as overstimulation compels the individual to assert their distinct identity during the interaction process. The progression unfolds in three stages: first, contextual interaction moderates the flow, ensuring sustained and genuine exposure along with balanced distribution within the psyche. Second, the balance tips into overexposure, severing the connection with the psyche's distribution and emphasizing the consciousness exposure. Third, there is a shift from mere exposure to a highly interactive experience—since continuous exposure would eventually overwhelm the individual, the psyche reconstructs the landscape.

At this juncture, the psyche disconnects from a real-time and direct exposure to consciousness and instead relies on a mental image that mirrors it, thereby sustaining interaction. This process is analogous to a cult leader who temporarily reintegrates with the subject's consciousness only to later detach, leaving behind an image that facilitates ongoing interactions.

This mental image, possessing qualities distinct from the initial exposure, is regarded as a memory rather than a current perception. Although the experience endures in perceptual time, the memory overlays the perceptual field, creating an impression of direct perception that is actually derived from a memory overlay. Since this memory is separate from the direct flow of consciousness, it remains accessible for engagement— albeit indirectly.

At this stage, interactions become volatile as the individual clings to the consciousness flow while a new aspect of the psyche takes command. This interactive component assumes dominance, and the potential for interaction becomes boundless. Consequently, the individual engages at such an intense level that they become overexerted—not from the exposure to consciousness but from excessive interaction— until they choose to leave the interaction altogether, allowing the process to begin anew.

A domestication near the center of conscious subjection will represent almost total embodiment of that flow. In this state, the domestication takes on the role of a stranger that presents a performative picture of the consciousness flow. The small interactive elements within are constantly at odds with one another, much like a well-known domesticity that, without choice, becomes mere representations of fame-related information.

To detach from this premise, the domestication must structurally separate rather than conceptually; only then can they interact with the particulars of their individuality. During their stay in that locality, they may momentarily depart from the conscious subjection, provided they are willing to do so. Yet it is difficult to conceptually detach from that subjection, as doing so would require disengaging from what is natural to the psyche and acting as if the structural presence were not there.

This is why context is so important—it already regulates the exposure. A highly contextual domestication has a built-in regulatory measure that allows its members to engage with the conscious subjection without being adversely affected. However, even this contextual domesticity continues to utilize representations, as each member adds nuance to the overall contextual premise.

The Highly Religious Domestication

A prime example is the highly religious domestication, where interactions among its members exist solely to represent the credence of that context. There is no interaction beyond that specific context, which explains why they are so willing to detach from members who do not meet their standards. They have separated themselves from the broader context, leaving no other realm of interaction to stimulate further engagement.

This type of domestication functions well near the center of conscious exposure because they already assume the role of representation, incorporating only certain conscious effects. It is common for identity groupings to be concentrated near the center locality, as they inherently include prerequisites that do not compromise the domestication or its exposure. The critique, however, lies in their structural formation from the onset, regardless of their chosen location.

The Domestication without Contextual Overlay

A domestication lacking a contextual overlay will represent each member based solely on consciousness exposure. In such cases, there is a constant hazard to the domestication's foundation—much like a prominent domesticity which appears only as representations of the conscious exposure without any intrinsic individuality. This fluidity is destabilizing for the domestication.

To counteract this, first, one must internally and conceptually engage with the consciousness exposure so that the domestication embodies both the consciousness and the context from which it arises. This approach allows the domesticative unit to be founded on a premise other than mere consciousness exposure—such as the institution of marriage serving as a contextual overlay. Naturally, that context is still partly influenced by the conscious subjection, as themes like relationships remain subject to its effects.

The second measure is to detach from the exposure and attempt to interact independently of its structural influence. We can convince ourselves or others that existence in its ordinary organism are sufficient without relying on consciousness.

Existence precedes consciousness—a fact that can be re-understood at any time to reveal a distinct human existence apart from its representation in sociality. Of course, plain existence cannot accomplish much without some attachment to consciousness, and immediately after detachment, reattachment tends to follow.

The third and most important measure is to structurally engage with localities that allow for interactive properties and to extend beyond the confines of the conscious subjection in order to obtain a more wholesome interactive exposure. There is no complete separation, but there are degrees to which one can shift toward a more interactive and less exposed state. The most detached state may be achieved geographically, politically, and socially, although such detachment might be harmful to the objective being pursued.

The Domestication outside the Center of Conscious subjection

When a domestication begins to engage slightly outside the center, changes occur. They do not adopt a complete representation of the exposure but rather capture select elements that reach its shores. In this locality, the reception of the exposure may include its most troubling aspects. The path of least resistance becomes the reception base, and the multitude of shadows turns into the primary exposure.

Such a locality can be considered the shadow of the center locality, as the exposed elements are not the prized material. Consequently, the domestication becomes a representation of these shadowed elements, with its members interacting primarily with the problematic aspects of the entire center locality. If one seeks to identify these problems, one need look no further than the sociality of this locality.

This situation presents both a problem and an opportunity for the domestication. The problem lies in the issues discussed above; the opportunity is that the domesticative members can interact with each other according to these representations, further developing these elements before reintroducing the resolved results into the center of exposure. Another, perhaps more significant approach is for the domestication to interact with the center locality on a regular basis—rejecting the structural offering and instead bringing home the center rather than the shadow it receives.

In a sense, this is common advice for all localities—to avoid shadow elements, one must continuously engage with the center. However, if one does so in a locality with little structural connection, then the consciousness will be grounded in that locality, further detaching it from the original premise. It becomes a cyclical movement, where consciousness is experienced locally, then reengineered as locally ordained, suggesting that it was the locality itself that provided the experience without its ongoing interaction with the center.

The Third Locality

The third locality remains structurally connected, though it does not receive a direct dosage of the consciousness flow and thus avoids exposure solely to shadow elements. This locality is coveted for its amenity because it provides wholesome exposure. However, one must remember that any exposure entering its confines is transferred through communication rather than direct contact. Without the accompanying sociality of a strong structural connection, what is received is merely hand-me-down exposure—a representation of the real thing that, over time, exerts its own effect.

If an individual or domestication does not reengage with the center or interact with a sociality that does, they will find themselves exposed. They might interact with the structural connection and partake in that exposure, but this would be merely a form of sociality based on physical items. With this understanding, it becomes clear why such a locality is prized: it claims to offer exposure—which is partly true—as well as an interactive environment with its inherent benefits. Yet when secondary exposure is well established, the interactive experience is diminished; without that connection, the interactive locality predominates. This locality oscillates constantly between being exposed during weekdays and becoming interactive on weekends.

Beneath the surface, however, this locality remains interactive only in its substructure. The exposed elements are not direct, despite the structural connection; they only provide a stable means of communicating the interaction. There is no genuine direct exposure—only a representation of it. The structural connection allows for adjustments to this representation, yet it remains a representation. A vast separation of political, social, and geophysical space prevents this locality from ever being directly exposed. That is why it does not receive the shadow; if it did, the center locality's shadow would always be present, undermining its intended function.

This situation also poses a problem: even if one attempts to physically engage with the center locality, they will be directed to continue using the representation they have always used. Because the representation is so effective, the individual may not be able to distinguish it from the real exposure and thus will engage with the center only from that perspective, never fully accessing the center and perpetually remaining in an interactive state. The difference between a representation and direct exposure is the difference between mere consciousness and a contextual overlay; even when not explicitly acknowledged, a contextual layer is always at work. Without it, exposure—typically granted by contextual layers—will be absent.

We may be tempted to consider this method as a means of avoiding exposure—a way to reconfigure the conscious subjection so that one can interact with it without the effects of exposure or irrelevant contextual information. However, without exposure, the final product is no different from a highly contextualized individual who appears unexposed.

The Center of Consciousness and Its Structural Implications

The center of consciousness is identifiable by its internal infrastructure, which emphasizes structural design over outgoing and incoming connections. Because it relies heavily on its internal system—sitting at its center and radiating outward—it depends on the sociality and movements within its internal environment.

The consciousness naturally gravitates toward a physical center, with the structural infrastructure emphasizing these elements and adapting according to the available sociality. In fact, the outgoing and incoming connections are often threadbare and underimposed due to the natural shadow buffer within the system. What is relevant for consciousness is largely irrelevant to what lies outside it, and little attention is given to the external infrastructure. Any sociality entering or leaving that domain does so through a representation of that shadow; if the light remains within, the shadow is what is transmitted outward.

The center of consciousness can deviate from its intended direction and fall into an interactive locality. This shift may occur suddenly due to environmental hazards, disruptions of normalcy and schedules, or other relevant causes. When this happens, the entire system enters a highly interactive state. This state is most apparent when the shadow domains become the primary material. The outgoing and incoming infrastructures become more significant, while the infrastructure providing internal sociality loses its prominence. All rules pertaining to interacting with local bodies apply equally to the center of consciousness. One can hardly imagine that, upon entering a state of interactive embodiment, there is no possibility of returning to the center of consciousness. Only with a significant footprint of sociality and the presence of regular infrastructure that provides a haven can one readily reenter the state of consciousness contemplation.

Upon exiting the consciousness encapsulation and shifting to an interactive state, all exposure comes to a standstill, and any dependencies, localities, or satellite cities lose their direct connection. One might even say that when the center of consciousness takes a break and enters a state of interactive embodiment, the entire system—including all that depends on civilization—loses its direct connection or its representation of consciousness.

It might be presumed that the influence of consciousness continues unabated because there is no discernible difference in structural reception. However, when we examine the differentiating aspects, it becomes clear that every direct connection turns into a representation; every representation depends on another representation. In this way, everyone is dependent on a memory of a previous state of encapsulated consciousness. Even within the locale itself, after downgrading to an interactive embodiment, the memory of the encapsulation remains so, that one may visit the locale and believe they are engaging with that—even though it has been downgraded.

The representation remains largely intact, and the memory is recent enough that an individual engaging with this locale feels as if they are experiencing an indirect relationship. Just as some locales do not engage directly but rely on a representation, so too does one who attempts to engage with this downgraded interactive embodiment.

What, then, is the difference between a representation based on communication without a structural connection and one based on a historical moment? When the memory of that conscious illumination is stretched so far that it enters a prolonged period of downgraded levels—even in direct connection—it depends on a wavering representation. Eventually, even the secondary reception loses its traction. Thus, if the center of consciousness loses its status for an extended period and becomes an interactive embodiment, not only is the direct relationship nearly lost, but every vulnerable, dependent locality is similarly downgraded. This could cause a great reset of the entire environment, as subtle changes eventually disrupt all conscious exposure, and civilization as a whole endures a gap in consciousness.

When a locality becomes disconnected from conscious discovery or loses its capacity because the exposure no longer permeates as it once did, the locality is downgraded to a lower stage of infrastructure. In time, most locales may be considered as deserts—where itemized representations are merely effects and, within the realm of conceptual databases, the locality is simply a desert in its entirety. This would force everyone into a conceptual realm, where no real interaction is demarcated by existence but is instead experienced as something contextual—

a research-based but ultimately irrelevant substitute for personhood or its sub-particles.

Therefore, a prolonged disruption of consciousness from the center locality would create a ripple effect, causing the entire civilization and its dependencies to either become lost in a conceptual and existential desert or be confined to a strict contextual space that disconnects them from true personhood. Upon reentry into conscious subjection, each locality would begin to shed its contextual domains and interact based on its original premises.

This scenario would produce an adverse ripple effect: rather than the consciousness dominating the sphere of influence, the overall contextual development would feed back into it, altering the nature of its consciousness. If the contextual reflections are part of a continuous conversation from when consciousness ceased, they might benefit, however, if the contextual developments do not follow any coherent conversation, it would create a troubling interaction that opposes the intended consciousness.

When there is conflict between conscious encapsulation and contextual development, the existential dynamics of the parties involved could lead to a restructuring of consciousness. This might result in a significant regression or the emergence of a new state of consciousness that may be largely irrelevant to authentic personhood. Because consciousness reaches its peak when aligned with existential personhood, any contextual development that deviates from that premise will lead to a form of vulnerability that lacks grounding in existential reality and becomes adversarial to both personal and global growth.

On Strangers and Social Interaction

A culture that encourages its citizens to expand their innate responses to the social system without recognizing limitations creates a social environment that labels unknown people as "strangers." These individuals are not seen as fellow citizens nor participants in a shared situation; they are perceived as the complete absence of existence—neither human nor animal, but as an undefined, dark entity.

The sight of them evokes a human form that represents a minor component of the social world. However, when interaction moves beyond neutrality, they are assumed to be non-existent, and even the representation of the public sphere is denied. In such an environment, passive interactions dominate to avoid becoming the person who actively engages, while still maintaining some semblance of sanity in an interactive world.

These passive interactions, both positive and negative, range from a slight nod or a forced smile to an empathetic glance. On the negative side, they include exhalations, inhalations, facial expressions of disgust, and rolling eyes—actions that replace genuine interaction and create a form of technical communication without dynamic engagement in a pronounced forum.

This behavior is not rooted in social anxiety but rather in a failure to recognize the full humanity of others in the midst of a social landscape. The "stranger" becomes the epitome of existential chaos, a symbol of disconnection, making any interaction to be a potentially troubling exposure. The solution is to engage without truly engaging—acknowledging the marginalized aspects of life without forcing substantial interaction, thereby avoiding dynamic change.

A simple exhale in a social setting may be perceived as a public judgment of one's own complacency. This happens despite the interaction being mediated through subversive means. The recipient of such behavior finds themselves in a compelling position—enticed by a high level of relationship engagement, albeit negative, yet unable to reciprocate or dismiss because no formatted interaction has occurred. The only way to approach is to recognize that the subversive interaction originates from someone uninterested in anything more complex.

Complacency, in this case, is not subject to question, nor is the possibility of a healthy interaction. The person who initiates the interaction has no concern for the generality of the being judged. The details that are highlighted are meant to boost the initiator's sense of existence within the social sphere. Thus, to properly reciprocate this interaction is to deliberately disregard the information they appear to convey. Regardless of whether the information is correct, and whether complacency can truly be recognized in one's subjective self, the interaction is not meant to foster change or truth. It serves only to affirm the initiator's existence within the social sphere, and the act of judgment aims to bolster their sense of being. The appropriate response, therefore, is to ignore the interaction and mark them as a stranger.

Rather than dismissing these normal social interactions as failures of humanity, those that are in relation to individuals involved, we could expand our intellectual perspective by ascribing a philosophy that compels this form of social interaction. The neutral social sphere is a blend of arising relationships and socially constructed interactions. The experience of these relationships in the public forum is determined by a singular factor: connection to the communal body and its representatives. Two people who have never interacted but are linked by a particular public situation are, in effect, interacting with each other as representatives of the larger public sphere. However, once the interaction becomes personal and private, they are removed from that shared relationship. Similarly, if their behavior becomes inconsistent, they cease to represent the public sphere, and the relationship reverts to one of stranger-to-stranger.

This is where the philosophy takes hold: by removing the public representative layer, we are thrust into an interaction that is purely strange. Under most other philosophies, relationships are governed by citizenship, communal agreements, and the political hierarchy embedded within those constructs. However, the philosophy of the centric locale does not impose citizenship or communal agreements, nor does it enforce a political hierarchy at the individual level. This is the central aim of the centric locale, which does not view its political system as a limiting institution but as an example of the limitless expanse of all existence.

If you seek a constitution that dictates certain ideals for individuals to adhere to, it cannot be found in the private interactions between citizens. The constitution is seen as an abstract concept that does not echo in the public sphere of daily life. For instance, one citizen cannot engage another by saying, "At least we agree on freedom," because the constitution hasn't entered the social sphere—doing so would suggest it is a limited text that will eventually lose its relevance. In fact, ordinary social interactions fail to align with the constitution or any communal agreement, and even citizenship may not be experienced as a common social institution. Therefore, instead of multiple layers of protection in social interactions, one is placed into complete strangeness, as if encountering someone without any political system above or between them.

Outskirts: Idealized Domestication, Public Intimacy, and Political Reality

Stateside culture is a valuable area of analysis when seeking to understand the political framework from which it emerges. At its core, outskirts is built upon the notion of domesticative ideals, which serves as a guiding principle. To be precise, it's impossible to imagine outskirts without domestication, and this connection forms the foundation that shapes its connotation.

The familial ideal within outskirts is characterized by the image of perfected domesticative units. There is little concern for the actual state of these families; rather, the focus is on presenting the domestication as a perceived ideal. Outskirts avoids delving into the true nature of familial dynamics because doing so would acknowledge the complications of domesticative life, which would undermine the political narrative that outskirts tries to project—one that is limitless in its scope.

The Paradox of Domestication in Outskirts

We intentionally refrain from engaging with the actual dynamics of domesticity because doing so would distance us from the political utopia that outskirts represents. However, there is an implicit recognition within outskirts that domesticity plays a crucial role in the progress of humanity. This ambivalence allows outskirts to embody domesticative ideals while simultaneously obscuring the true nature of domesticity. This portrayal of domestication allows individuals to embrace the image of their domesticity while participating in the expansive political ideology that outskirts represents. The domestication, idealized as an example, is then thrust into the public sphere: "As I enjoy this domesticity, so should you." Though this may seem ironic, as most people wouldn't want others to engage with their domestication in the same way they do, when domestication is seen merely as an example, the external world is compelled to partake.

Stateside children are raised within this paradox, accepting the notion that the idealization of domestication carries a certain importance. Every domesticative unit that participates in the public eye is transformed into that very example. Just as an individual who meets a noteworthy person might find their own identity shaped by that encounter, so too does the stateside domesticative unit become a public affair, especially when unified, allowing it to be recognized as universally significant.

This creates a situation where families begin to see themselves as the definitive reality of all existence. While this is not the true reality, when something private becomes public, it is assumed to encompass the entire public sphere. The experience of such exposure makes families cautious about where and with whom they interact, especially in public, as they strive to present themselves in the most favorable light for future progress.

Moreover, the true nature of domestication is that it functions as an example, even if it is biologically validated. As an example, domestication's purpose is to showcase itself, not to engage in existential participation. When a domestication attempts to engage existentially or claims to be the only reality, it begins to interact in a way that excludes the individuals within domestication, leading to a superficial and underwhelming exchange.

True relationships, it seems, are rooted in the avoidance of existential engagement because once such a connection occurs, it becomes impossible to relate in the same way. When outskirts idealizes domestication, it risks undermining the deeper concept of relationships, reducing them to mere teaching moments. These moments can only occur when domestication is seen as an example to teach human progress. Once the example becomes a reality in and of itself, it no longer serves a pedagogical function—it simply encompasses the entire state of being.

As mentioned earlier, many true aspects are highlighted in outskirts' version of domesticity. One significant element is that, in typical domesticative situations, interactions between families are not encouraged, as they are seen as belonging to an external and unknown realm. Within outskirts, the domesticative unit operates under the political umbrella of outskirts, which emphasizes domesticative ideals. Thus, the entire domestication thrives under the influence of outskirts, following its prescribed movements. The neighbor is, in a sense, an extension of one's domesticity because both exist within the domain of outskirts, which places value on domestication.

This creates an environment where familial affairs become public, allowing other families and individuals to participate. When intimacy is shared in one domesticity, the entire neighborhood can benefit from that experience. Similarly, the reverse is true: intimacy is extended to the neighbors because they are part of the "familial unit" for which outskirts represents. A domestication is only possible because of outskirts, and as long as there is a clear understanding of outskirts which incorporates the people of a town or city, domestication draws its energy from that larger system. To claim ownership of a domesticative unit, one must surpass the complex conceptualization of the particular outskirts in which they reside. This can be understood when the stateside fails to manifest a cohesive understanding, resulting in an inconsistency within the households of that domain.

When the intimacy of one neighbor is shared with others, it fosters a sense of unity that spreads further and further. If this process occurs consistently throughout outskirts, the connection to the broader community—whether a town or city—becomes deeply intimate. However, this sense of intimacy within stateside walls often fades when compared to external connections. This is because the entire stateside system is dependent on the political structures that surround it. When that attachment weakens, what exists within the walls of outskirts will not be experienced as reality.

Outskirts' Idealized Domestication and its Limitations

Similar to a domesticative unit that has achieved intimacy in its private domain while remaining disconnected from external reality, such intimacy holds a certain authenticity but becomes diluted as its attachment to the outside world increases.

When intimacy within the outskirts remains detached from political reality, it transforms into a costly form of intimacy. This detachment is akin to infidelity—an experience that may seem fulfilling in the short term but ultimately disrupts the broader social system.

Nevertheless, the outskirts offer a level of intimacy that cannot be found elsewhere. This refers to the familial unit, rooted in biological connections, which consistently provides a deeper familiarity. However, this form of intimacy can foster a desire to remain attached solely to this particular level, dismissing other aspects of reality—much like how infidelity neglects the potential for deeper connections.

Outskirts' relationship to wider political realities can be examined at both individual and governmental levels. At the individual level, people can engage with the larger political world in ways that compensate for its limitations. With sufficient participation, attachment to these systems naturally strengthens. At the governmental level, this engagement is evident through political actions, commerce, law, and public representation. These mechanisms form the foundation of diplomatic relations—encompassing the exchange of goods, services, legal interactions, and public media.

One reason to encourage external participation is to legitimize domestication as an entity. Since the outskirts is a political construct that shapes reality, domestication must reflect that reality. However, merely constructing and assuming it to be real does not make it so; this drives individuals to seek external recognition of their familial existence.

This does not fully explain why domestication must be idealized. It can be understood through the natural tendency of individuals to position themselves within their domesticative structure. Rather than merely observing domestication as an example, individuals are intimately and existentially engaged with it. This engagement leads to the idealization of domestication as an expression of selfhood. People desire to be seen in the best possible light, especially when they gain the impression that their character is underdeveloped.

Idealizing domestication as a model implies that it is more than just a functional unit. The true nature of familial attachment runs deeper. The underlying fear in the outskirts is not a wish for an improved domesticative unit but a drive to prove one's connection to the political reality for which domestication represents. This drive serves to demonstrate a perfected character through one's existential attachment to the familial ideal. The greatest achievement in the outskirts is to appear both attached and detached—to show membership in the political reality while also embracing domestication as an ideal.

The highest source of shame in the outskirts is a domestication which appears dysfunctional, as it exposes humanity's limitations and represents the greatest form of political ugliness. Each individual and their familial role serve as a public representation of the self. Although the true essence of the individual is often hidden, within the outskirts the individual is expected to be exemplified through domestication. The system upholds certain true ideals regarding familial reality, and its members strive not to contradict the prevailing political reality. As a result, individuals work to appear as though they are not overly attached to the domesticative unit.

The domesticative unit is idealized to appear perfect, thereby preventing any unease in the public perception of humanity's true nature. A milder form of shame would be to appear excessively existentially attached to the familial body, but this is often too subtle for the public to notice. However, an encounter with one in such a position would bring this shame to light—especially if they meet a more efficacious acquaintance. The natural response is then to prove one's own achievements, independent of the domesticative unit.

This dynamic leads to a highly structured form of parenting within the household—a performative act aimed at exemplary results. This parenting occurs solely within the confines of the home, ensuring that it never appears as though domestication is acting under external imposition. The impression given is that domestication would act this way without external oversight. Public parenting is strongly discouraged in the outskirts, as it reveals existential attachment and human limitations. The very act of parenting, when infused with existential concern, demonstrates that domestication is the only reality in the situation.

What may seem like socialization in the outskirts is, in reality, strict instruction aimed at producing exemplary public behavior. There is little interest in private activities unless they contribute to this public exemplification. When private activities become public, domestication faces severe condemnation—not for the individual, but for the failure to exemplify the ideal.

The outskirts should not be reduced to a mere facade; it does offer certain benefits. Although it may not seek familial ideals in their most fundamental sense, the outskirts uphold domestication as its core ideal, thereby ensuring adherence to the structured domesticative model. This, in turn, convinces the public of its legitimacy—a process that requires a vast system of support. Through these mechanisms, true domesticative ideals eventually emerge, representing the great benefit of a stateside life.

However, this benefit requires a community of people who can access and appreciate true aspects of familial life. The outskirts are generally not equipped to foster a communal experience, making it difficult for a particular private experience to be completely disconnected from that of others. When a structured community does exist, it enables each domesticity to develop independently and, secondarily, to mediate when the outskirts' conceptualization is absent—thus serving as an additional channel for community unification.

Navigating Between Personal Singularity and Universal Centers

This framework allows for a balance between detachment from preset systems and active participation in their interactions. By maintaining two frames of reference—one based on the present situation and the other on a broader, more detached identity—each can serve to balance the other. When progress is sought, one may refer to the appropriate frame:

using the detached identity to reflect on the current situation, or the present context to inform one's identity.

Through such contrasts, we can distinguish the characteristics that define each frame, allowing for a thorough analysis. For instance, an identity might promote participation in community enterprises, a notion that can be contrasted with a stateside locale which may not support such enterprises. In some cases, community enterprises reflect specific stateside conditions while also incorporating the outskirts' emphasis on the individual realm—thus preventing overindulgence in community and ensuring that each frame checks the other.

The Importance of Relational Reflection

As reflection deepens, one may explore the reasons behind communal adherence versus the outskirts' focus on the individual. Through such deliberation, a more coherent understanding emerges, leading to more informed practical decisions.

Communities of this nature are rare in the outskirts because they require an environment that nurtures intimate interactions. While schooling might serve as one method of fostering these interactions, it often falls short of establishing continuous dialogue. When the outskirts manage to create a community that offers the necessary intimacy, that community becomes a habitat that even non-stateside areas may lack.

Entering such an establishment may cause one's self-perception to shift to that of residing on an isolated island—a place where one is the sole member. Other residents become mere aesthetics, and genuine human contact is called into question. One may feel centered, as if inhabiting a one-person island, yet also sense another center that cannot be pinpointed to any single individual. This center is experienced as a collective whole—a sense of preservation that emerges not solely from personal identity, but from an intermingling of the self with the collective.

Many mistakenly assume that interaction with high-status figures or political leaders equates to engaging with this true center. The error lies in the fact that when one is unable to access an essential component, the next reference becomes merely a representation or an example. However, the isolation of a singular representation detaches one from the true center and fails to serve as an adequate substitute. For example, encountering someone from the upper strata might give the illusion of engaging with the center; in reality, such an interaction only distances one further from the complete center, offering merely a fragment of its significance. To truly engage with the center, one must recognize its capacity and complexity—qualities that any single representation is bound to deflect.

The Role of Relational Value in Connecting to the Center

There is one element that can reconcile this paradox: the relational element. This component can interact with both the center and any specific representation of interest. In any given encounter, the relational element highlights aspects that transcend the singularity of the event. Unlike a singular representation that stands solely for a greater reality, relational value embeds the interaction within a larger context. It de-emphasizes the uniqueness of that particular event, expanding personhood to include the interaction without subordinating selfhood.

For instance, in a romantic engagement, one tends to select an environment that embodies the majority of relational value, thereby incorporating the entirety of the external center. This integration continues as long as the chain of singular events remains focused on the relational value that encompasses all known reality—a value that does not remain tethered to its singular namesake.

When a setting fails to acknowledge its incorporation into a larger reality, it is experienced merely as a singularity. Similarly, attempting to relate to a conglomerate of singularities as if it were a universal nexus risks undermining one's own personhood. The universal center is part of each person; however, positioning it as an isolated singularity causes one to lose connection to the factual center, reducing it to mere information about an assumed center. This does not occur with a true center, because comprehensiveness only leads to further comprehensiveness without constraining personhood. When an individual identifies with this true center, their personal, singular aspects naturally follow as the data for all future interactions. The true center thus allows the singularity of the person to develop without limitation.

In contrast, the false center—being a true singularity— integrates into personhood as an assumed universal center. It begins to dictate that personal aspects follow and receive input only from this singular data point. This results in a decline of personhood, wherein the individual is bound to a fabricated universality that contains limited data and resists perceiving beyond that constrained reality.

The True Center and Its Expansive Nature

The true center possesses expansive data and remains open to perceiving a wholeness greater than itself. Even if the available data seems limited, there is always the possibility of more because the true center is bound to its own legitimacy rather than being confined by it. It recognizes its historical precedent—acknowledging that there was once a time when it was not centered at all—and it accepts the potential to become more or less centered in the future. The process of centering to a higher degree requires incorporating what lies beyond, striving to receive all available data points of reality regardless of their labels, all in a spirit of humility.

There may be cases where relational value does not capture the full breadth of known reality. For instance, familial bonds carry high relational value yet remain deeply personal and are not easily understood as representing the wholeness of known reality. Equating a familial attachment with something as impersonal as a public kiosk—a mere relational marker in the urban landscape—would be a significant mental leap. Unlike the kiosk, which does not demand personal interaction and is experienced as a singularity, familial bonds are biologically and emotionally charged to be severely personal.

A domesticative member, when assumed to be an element of wholeness devoid of singularity, reflects a reaction to self-perception. This self-perception fails to recognize its personal basis, that is, instead of viewing the domesticative member as one might view a kiosk in a city. Such a view contradicts the notion of self-preservation and may lead to the infamous self-sacrifice associated with romantic ideals, while also neglecting the true sense of self.

By nature, a human is a singularity in the truest sense—primarily due to residing within one's own unique system. When we remove the center of selfhood in favor of an enlarged center, both are lost; there would be no individual available for interaction when everything were subsumed under one whole center. Interaction, by definition, involves two parts: the reception of the interaction and the interacting material. As noted in other works, the true romantic ideal is painfully aware of this duality.

The Paradox of Isolation and Interaction

One thus encounters interactions that are inherently singular. This perspective reflects the centered self and its various components. It accepts that an alternative center exists outside oneself while also incorporating oneself. This external center may manifest through relational aspects that recognize one's inclusion within it.

In this mode of thought, every interaction is seen through the lens of the whole center. For example, a kiosk is not viewed as a singularity because one is engaging in a reflective mode that does not reduce selfhood to singularity. In interactions with a domesticative member, the personal aspect is unmistakably present. By contrast, when interacting with a kiosk, the personal element is consciously minimized—even though such a minimization is almost inevitable. It is as if one views the interaction from a detached, third-party perspective, where the singularity of selfhood is absent.

Familial attachment contain an element of the universal center, discernible to an intuitive mind. However, when interacting within the context of a familial bond, one considers the universal aspect in contrast to singularity. A domesticative member might embody a specific disposition of the world: a product of their era, a particular personality type, a feminine or masculine inclination, a response to societal injustice, a reaction to corrective action across generations, or a manifestation of psychological processes intertwined with universal familial elements. The argument is that the most intricate familial attachments inherently contain universal responses.

Problems arise when familial attachments, experienced as singularities, are misinterpreted as external centers. This is particularly evident in the evolution of a child, who initially perceives domestication as both their subjective center and an external center. A child may assume that their experiences constitute the entirety of reality. When a parent expresses anger, for example, the child may feel that the entire structure of reality is suffused with anger. Yet, while the angry parent represents a specific emotional state, it is important not to generalize this state to encompass all possible experiences. In reality, the moment of anger contains only a limited set of data compared to the broader reality; treating it as all-encompassing reduces one's perspective to a narrow scope.

Universalizing an experience instead of expanding the underlying emotion (such as anger) exclusively initiates the process of relating to the absolute center. The parent, as an angry respondent from a former generation or personality type, represents an interaction with the entirety of human psychology and societal dynamics at its behest. This mediation is not reached through the study of anger alone, but through a broader exploration of psychological or societal ideas.

The Interplay of Singularities and Universal Centers

Analyzing the interaction itself can be effective, but only within the constraints of a universal expansion, one which personhood has experienced. This becomes particularly important when one is prompted to meditate on universal themes alongside singular experiences. Such mediation is accessible by investigating into the depth of relational material, which channels residual universal themes that have yet to interact. However, if one attempts to extract more details than what is readily available, that strand of interaction may be misinterpreted as universality, thereby diminishing genuine reality.

Innovative learning is then integrated into its appropriate domain within the realm of singularities. For example, parents become embodiments of new material in light of their intrinsic connection to it. The parent evolves into an avatar of society—a dynamic system influencing everyone—and can be seen as a representation of an entire generation. These connections are undeniable; even when a parent acts from a singular reference point in a specific scenario, they remain influenced by all these broader connections.

Thus, every being emanates partially from the absolute center and dually from their personal singularity. The absolute center holds objective truth for the entire Earth and its history—a claim that could extend even to our galaxy and beyond, as its influence does not abruptly cease. While a black hole might represent a point where influence is significantly diminished, the innermost contents still retain a degree of influence, albeit diminished.

This relationship might suggest that a black hole is connected either to the absolute center of Earth or to a competing center in an alternative habitat. The lowest point of influence should not be assumed to be a realm of nothingness; rather interacting with the highest point. Just as the highest point of influence carries the greatest existential risk—a kind of nothingness—the lowest point, exhibiting similar characteristics, should also interact. Although the integration of influence requires some degree of it, a point of non-influence would not serve as a contender for the highest degree.

Naturally, if the absolute center were to expand such that its existential margin allowed passage through the black hole, time and space might be minimized, and nature could be manipulated from that vantage point. Yet, such control would be purposeless if it resulted in a mental state of nothingness, devoid of a distinct agenda. An external force might harness one's state for its own ends, but this would necessitate deep interaction by means of personal identity. In such scenarios, relationships between individuals often involve one person acting as the harness while the other a being harnessed—a dynamic that merits further exploration.

The State, Communication, and the Dissemination of the Center

A state or state that happens to host that center may exemplify that status to ascertain its reality to distribute its information; as well, they may seek to continue its center by demanding a certain responsibility from the citizen for maintaining it. Despite what seems like isolationist domains, the interaction through every possible medium will distribute the information with effectiveness.

Through subtle human and animal communication, plant life, and weather formations, they will prove able-bodied to transmit the data of the absolute center. Unless the isolation detaches from atmospheric influence, it will be a part of this system. The information that transmits through non-conscious mediums will contain a fine subconscious thread that will be adequate for the transfer of material. When we further analyze, we would find that even what we can term personal is still a universal manifestation. There are no fundamental elements that are genuinely personal; however, in reacting to our unavoidable situation of being bound to our own existence, we must create a personal domain. This is only in service to approach that universality so that the home is only to experience more society; context is only to receive more universality; domestication is only to interact with all beings.

The safety experience from the home is only the intermediate experience of interacting with one's singularity, which is only a method for accessing supplementary universality beyond the home. With only the focus on reaching that singularity devoid of any expansion, it will decrease the experience of itself. Technically, one will decline their capacity to interact with their singularity until they fall into the background of a universal system that will make use of them. This would be in respect to how we view elements of nature as acting as a form of nature, missing any singularity of their inherent systems.

The slave loses their singularity and partakes in the universal system that surrounds them. We understand the contentiousness of the subject, being that slavery and perfective forms of servitude are symptoms of an exploding absolute center that overrides the personal realm. This continues unless equipped to interact with such an intense center. For the periods of history with the largest absolute center will always be filled with a strong loss of the personal realm, with slavery as a manifestation, and a great need for a competent homebody.

This is because the homebody will be able to remain stalwart to continue the interactions with central universality without succumbing to either complete universality like the slave or no universality like the degenerate outcast. The theme of slavery and the homebody would indicate an expansive absolute center that requires a finer degree of tuning. The slavery aspect is its vulnerability in the populace for being unable to maintain the personal realm, either from those who are able to assist or the failed populace who have diminished. The homebody aspect serves as the remedy for offering the ability to revert the effects of that failure. The competent homebody is the subject of another work that deserves much attention.

In some sense, instead of viewing them as lacking the context/home/singularity, we can view them as lacking a locale onto which they can interact with the environment that they are part of. The lack of home is not the loss; it is the lack of a plateau from which to interact with universality. Homelessness is always a city problem, for they become the universality of the system without an available locale to interact with it from another vantage point. Outside of the city, they will not require a proficient locale as the system is not universal or complex. We can term it homelessness amongst universality; while outside the city, it would be simply lacking shelter. We arrive at the conclusion that outside the city, whatever appears to be a home is not fundamentally such. That is, unless the members partake in the universal system of the city in some fashion. At face value, everybody in outskirts is homeless yet contains shelter. When the home becomes a necessity is when the absolute universality of all of reality is sought out, which would be the city and its connection to the hierarchy of cities under the most expansive universal system.

Within the kiosk, the singularity themes, such as the personal interactions devoid of the center at large, although being an element of truth, are not the majority of the interaction. The kiosk exists only in response to participating in the center, for it exemplifies its surrounding environment. The people who reside in the kiosk have understood their role in that larger center preceding their personal basis that may be present. The entire system is more inclined towards the true center than when personal interaction is experienced; it is a residual effect of the failure of the participants in recognizing that. When it becomes highly personal, then it will remove the environment and center from the interaction and take the role of a singularity interaction. At intervals, the entrance into singularity grants a certain stableness to the individuals who are otherwise lost within the true center. At other intervals, such an interaction would be troubling due to the willingness to interact with the true center while proponents are compelling them to depart from it.

As human representation is limited to provide this function, the location for which the center resides will not have a limitation. There is no singularity in the location that doesn't threaten to detach from the center, and the wholeness only seeks to include more wholeness.

Part 2:

The Interactive Embodied Environment: Psychic Parts and Domesticative systems.

An interesting phenomenon within the *interactive embodied environment* is that an individual may find it difficult to initiate a breakdown of their interactive layers. Theoretically speaking, this process is therapeutically similar to embarking on a journey that disrupts the path toward present amelioration and the wholeness of personhood, as it focuses on specific psychic parts. The *interactive embodied environment*, being both interactive and politically embodied, transforms into a performance of the present moment, characterized by a cyclical journey.

Within conscious subjection—or any designated locale, even that of the domestication—there is no performance that involves the breakdown of psychic parts. In that subjection, the process does not extend into ritualistic specifics. Instead, it serves as a through-line, where one simply attaches to any point along the hierarchy within that linear structure. Therefore, when embarking on a therapeutic journey that emphasizes breakdowns of the present moment, individuals need only attach to different portions of the consciousness continuum that correspond with their newly developed personality.

However, upon entering an *interactive embodied environment*, the fragmented psychic parts evolve into new information, following the through-line and creating a continuous performance of these elements. Instead of advancing toward a segment of the political continuum, the *interactive embodied environment* lacks such an amenity and compels any psychic part to become receptive, initiating its socialization within that locale. This is frequently observed within the domestication, where a therapeutic journey immediately conflicts with the unit. Domestication begins interacting with the psychic part, even though it represents only one facet of a comprehensive person.

Theoretically, it could be argued that it is impossible to break down psychic parts while simultaneously engaging in real-time interactions with the domestication. Even if this were possible, the domestication would only emphasize those psychic parts at the expense of the person's wholeness, contradicting true well-being. In fact, the domestication might even turn against the person's wholeness in order to maintain its usual interactions with psychic parts that are archaic and irrelevant to a complete sense of self. Interaction, after all, is indifferent to what it engages with; it assumes that it substantiates wholesome personhood.

Even the individual may fail to notice that they are treading a path where sociality is determined to resurrect what is buried in historical memory—a dormant psychic shadow. The difference between the domestication and the *interactive embodied environment*, in this regard, is that the latter functions as a political system. It drags dormant psychic parts into the public sphere and creates a framework for the individual that disconnects from wholesome personhood. In contrast, the domestication is confined to a non-political structure, offering the advantage of providing a framework that does not demand a rigid reality but instead encourages localized and domesticated interaction.

This leads to the difficulty in realizing and actualizing a singular reality structure, where therapeutic disintegration and compartmentalization become adversarial. Since the domestication is considered the only reality structure, it is believed that all interactions represent the final determination of existence, coupled with interactive substances of personhood that remained dormant or repressed. Thus, the domestication continues its interactions in every recognized domain, ultimately threatening one's existence, appropriating, actualizing, and degenerating the wholeness of personhood.

Two protective measures guard against this phenomenon within the domestication. First, it is essential to clearly recognize that the domestication is not a reality structure but a domestication of a localized system. This ensures that interactions remain external, rather than permeating all aspects of personhood. The second measure is to establish a clear separation between the individual and their interactions with the domestication—especially during the disintegration of psychic parts—so these parts can be regulated and developed, ultimately merging to re-establish wholesome personhood before any further interaction with the domestication. This results in two related elements: first, a separation of the domestication from the overarching reality structure or political spectrum; and second, a separation of the individual from the domestication, recognizing their proper place and role in the world.

The *interactive embodied environment* differs because separating its structure from the political addendum inherent in universality is more difficult to recognize and implement. While it is easy to acknowledge that domestication is merely a definition, it becomes especially challenging when an entire system—even a political one—must be recognized as a sophisticated form of domestication. The second protective measure, as discussed, is the clear demarcation between the individual's disintegration of psychic parts and their interaction with such a locale—a separation that is more difficult to achieve within it than outside of it.

Because it is politically propagating, even if one recognizes the locale's separation from reality, an individual will still be unable to extricate themselves from its pervasive dominion. Within that locale, where could one go without being exposed to its sociality? If one conceptually separates at the moment of disjunction, the subjection only serves to expose them further. This is why it is difficult to separate from consciousness itself. The most thorough attempt at separation is detrimental to the psyche because, immediately afterward, consciousness attempts to reintegrate, necessitating alternative methods rather than mere theoretical separation.

The process of establishing a domain in an *interactive embodied environment* is complex because it proceeds throughout the system, even permeating the household. While certain domains thrive in this setting and attempt to engage with the *interactive embodied environment* in a broader sense—seeking to augment their constitution to be perpetuated throughout their social sphere—neglecting the prospect of a domain designed to shadow and shy away from public exposure only creates additional domains that overwhelm the *interactive embodied environment*.

Providing the service of a private domain that detaches from public exposure would require de-establishing the locale as interactive altogether. If the domestication serves its most regular function as an interactive locale, there is a method to protect its interaction from becoming overly embodied, given the substance of the immediate external locale. However, promoting the domestication to be something other than interactive is divisive and requires careful consideration of both its utility and necessity.

First, consider its purpose: domestication provides something the public in this locale fails to offer—a counter to the notion that the public is merely a series of interactions lacking a connection to consciousness. The constitution of the domestication, then, would involve reimagining the public not as a fundamentally undefined entity but as a nuanced detail of interaction that neither defines reality nor necessitates social movement. This perspective allows the domestication to serve as a lens through which the locale—already established as a non-entity—can be connected to a particular social reality of interaction, enabling individual growth.

Equipped with this contextual layer, domestication has the resources to interact with the public domain, reinforcing internalized interactions based on a consciousness otherwise absent in this locale. For example, if the context lacks any service or regulation from the consciousness center, then upon reuniting with that center, all the gains made in the interactive locale will be lost. Moreover, it will create a "halo effect" that misleads the individual's understanding of the consciousness center. This, in turn, leads to a further decline in the new contextual layer within the *interactive embodied environment*, perpetuating the cycle until no consciousness remains in the domestication—even after the journey to the central locale.

The Interactive Locale— Exhausted Data Center

This locale, due to its severance from the central entity, exists in an exhaustible state. This condition functions to domesticate aspects of the non-domesticated elements beyond its boundary. The stamina of this exhaustion process depends on how effectively it retains its representation of a more realistic substance. Once that representation begins to appear substantial in its own right, it reaches its exhaustible limit. This process may unfold over minutes or days, depending on the volume of material flowing from the representation. When the material is present in low dosage, the representation is used less, reducing its capacity to function solely as a bridge to reality.

The degree of this material is determined by its appropriation of psychic elements—a high degree of material results in an existential demarcation. A researcher residing in a remote interactive locale, for instance, can continue their work despite relying on the same representation for their conscious connection. They achieve this by employing a contextual layer, as their research poses no existential vulnerability. Only through the stability of this contextual mindset can their work.

The Process of Exhaustion

Existential vulnerability is enabled by the part of the individual that seeks out that climate, or is afforded by circumstance. For instance, a traumatic episode—always marked by existential vulnerability—exhausts the interactive locale for immediate reparation. After such an episode, or after the emphasis on one, there is often a period of exploration beyond the fringes of the interactive locale, where the trauma (or, in our terms, explosive material) has exhausted the system. The interactive locale may be attributed for overexposing the individual to information, as it was not equipped to handle such an expansion. This is, after all, the inherent nature of the interactive locale. What manifests as resentment is the belief that the interactive locale was responsible for more than it could offer, that the homebody was presumed to be a true reality structure when, in fact, it remained merely the most potent interactive locale.

This belief is an element of every infantile locale, which falsely assumes its interactive structure to be a reality structure. Thus, it is only through the proper method of growth that one harbors resentment, and the shame and avoidance of that recognition might mark a period of delay in the maturity stage—even when growth is pressing. Alternatively, it might be that the very nature of the infantile-to-maturity process is in question—perhaps a method of self-destruction that leads the individual to believe they possessed the ability for maturity but was not comprehensive. Instead of presuming a failure of movement, it is a letdown to recognize the humanistic process that requires the transitory period from infantile stages to mature ones.

The exhaustion is evident when the interactive locale—experienced subjectively as the reality structure—forms the belief that its experience is thoroughly true. Anything beyond its boundaries is seen as suspect, contradictory to the "reality." External elements are considered arbitrary, while what is experienced within the locale is deemed substantial. There is subjective evidence on its side, for the current experience is seemingly factual and the intimacy thorough and binding, while what lies outside may not be experienced at all or is experienced differently in the current mindset of possibility.

Cognition and the Interactive Locale

Even as normal exhaustion comes at the cost of an adversarial element—a reprisal for interaction—this exhaustion is unrelenting when the reality structure is presumed to be the psyche itself. Resentment arises at the level of emotional organization when this exhausted state is recognized. However, cognition remains unaffected, as it is bound to reality structures. As long as there is an adapted locale to produce it, cognition remains at ease. The psyche itself is not exhausted, as the interactive locale is not produced from a material existential vulnerability. Even though intimacy is experienced, it is ultimately an external entity presiding over a person without requiring the existential movement typical of genuine existential vulnerability.

When the interactive locale becomes exhausted, the entire psyche shifts into a compartmentalized state, where all new material is experienced as a conceptual database. The intimacy within the locale becomes a signaling reward for continuity, whereas the psyche begins to decommission its unused parts. Though the interactive locale is presumed to be the reality structure, it now functions as a contextual aspect that gains prominence over the entirety of the psyche.

The Disparity between Internal and External Realities

We must ask why the supposed reality structure of the psyche does not apply to existential formation, despite being supposed to represent the system's reality. This arises because existential formation does not function as an internal mechanism; rather, it is outsourced to an external reality away from the individual. When the psyche perceives a disparity between its internal reality structure and authentic external reality, it becomes dependent on the external system for existential validation. In doing so, the psyche identifies itself merely as a mechanism for interacting with a more genuine external structure.

The decommissioning of the psyche reflects this internal disparity. It replicates itself like a textbook—static and unchanging—rather than as a living, social being. The textbook becomes a contextual database, lacking dynamic flow or relational reciprocity with its content, and the psyche begins to function in a similar manner. Any content relevant to existential formation is proposed by an external mechanism, rendering access difficult. This resembles a person so thoroughly contextualized that social interaction recedes from the foreground of experience and, when it does occur, it is highly distilled.

The child initially assumes domestication to be their reality structure nevertheless begins to decommission large portions of their psyche upon intuitively recognizing that this structure does not align with genuine reality. Even without the intellectual tools to grasp external information, the child senses that their presumed reality is incomplete. This ability does not depend on external input; rather, it stems from the internal mechanism being a self-contained encapsulation of substance that recognizes its own displacement from the center of reality.

To illustrate: if consciousness and the capacity for subjective experience are imagined as a liquid streaming from an external center, then as this liquid travels to the fringes and ends in domestication, it identifies itself through this very process. Its voice and DNA carry the imprint of being a dosage—something extracted and transmitted through various stages. Upon receiving this liquid, the child absorbs both its identity and its substance. As a result, the child does not *intuitively* grasp the limitations of their reality structure; instead, they receive the information already shaped by that structure. What appears as intuition is, in fact, a default consequence of the child's psyche lacking the tools to recognize external information.

The conscious reception in a child's psyche is always auxiliary and contextually framed, unlike that of an adult. The child's reality structure is further removed from the external world. As maturity transpires, contextual categories dissolve, making way for a more individualized form of existential interdependence—where internal and external realities begin to align. The more they align, the more independent existential formation becomes.

This is why education is fundamentally an infantile notion—it leads toward a stage of maturity that transcends its initial boundaries. In maturity, existential formation becomes less dependent on contextual framing. Even so, the mature individual still requires context for interaction, as individuality inherently involves being a distinct being, not merely a composite of collective consciousness.

The furthest an individual can advance without the psyche becoming dysfunctional lies in a grade that permits sufficient existential interaction without drifting too far from authentic external reality. This is evident in relationships: for example, it is inappropriate for an adult stranger to interact with a child freestanding of a contextual framework, such as that of a teacher. The child, being further removed from the center of reality, prerequisites this buffer. Without a defined context, the adult risks becoming absorbed into the child's incomplete reality structure—even if their own is more developed.

Within the *interactive embodied environment*, there exists a maximum threshold for interaction—beyond which integration fails. Outside this threshold lies the domain of central consciousness: a realm relevant to representation, but no longer participating directly in the continuity of consciousness. Upon entering an *interactive embodied environment*, the structure distinguishes itself by disrupting this continuity in order to reflect upon interactivity. Domestication functions in a similar way—distancing itself from the public sphere to embed interaction within the private realm.

In political systems that marginalize forms of sociality which are not directly connected to consciousness, the dominant mode becomes one that disregards its own foundations. It focuses only on what is immediately observable. In these systems, a substructure emerges that creates communal spaces where individuals observe one another for both validation and signs of disruption. Suspicion often dominates such environments: members, especially those in influential positions, subconsciously act as sentinels guarding the flow of consciousness.

Subcultures emerge within this layered context of interactivity. While the standard locale represents a universal embodiment that expands without fixed direction, it still retains political aspects. Though aspiring toward universality, it remains reliant on the political spectrum. It depends on the flow of political consciousness to transmit its information interactively. The degree to which universality can exist beyond the political depends on how the political system interacts with it.

Support from an interactive locale arises when certain social elements enter its domain, carrying a form of conscious encapsulation independent of the prevailing political spectrum. This allows the locale to serve as a more authentic and complete embodiment of universality. Yet beneath this lies the potential for sub-contextual layers, permitting various forms of interaction. These locales may seem detached from the political spectrum, but upon closer examination, they are often subcultures perpetuating the same genre of interactivity—aligning with select political elements while failing to embrace the whole spectrum. This becomes problematic, as such interactivity lacks a direct connection to consciousness and instead relies on a fragment of the political system—forming only a secondary connection. Consequently, interactivity loses its final link to conscious receptivity.

Since the locale is both dependent on and receptive to the political spectrum, experiences within it are generally true to consciousness. Yet no individual experiences existential loss unless interactions detach from consciousness or hinder its continuous reconnection.

This is why locales attempting to embody the political spectrum—often through symbols, flags, or creeds—frequently fail to reconnect to consciousness. Their loss results from having constructed a secondary *interactive environment* that, from inception, was disconnected from consciousness. Although it may appear direct—perhaps even more so—the political spectrum is already permeating the space, creating a duplicate interactive environment. Ironically, such locales are often the most distant from both the political spectrum and consciousness; for without consciousness, the political spectrum is lost.

This is why church and state cannot be constructed as a singular system. A unified system would merge the political spectrum with religion, turning religion into an interactive environment aimed at the political realm—thus creating a secondary connection, severing its link to consciousness. When religion is separated from the state, it can function as an interactive locale that fosters consciousness directly. But once it becomes a state addendum, it must pass through two layers to reach consciousness, rendering it inauthentic both in terms of consciousness and interactivity. Thus, church and state cannot be unified; if the church is to serve as a vessel for consciousness.

We can assess whether an *interactive environment* is of a first-degree relation (true interactivity with consciousness) or a second-degree (a foundered experience of consciousness) based on the way it separates itself from what lies beyond its limits. When the separation occurs in a clear and disruptive manner, we must assume that consciousness does not permeate naturally through its culture; rather, the enclosures represent its secondary nature. For the genuine interactive locale is sensitive, dependent, and vulnerable to its connection to consciousness and would never take an extreme in that regard—even if it does in any other respect. That very balance allows it to be an interactive invited locale; the moment it reaches any extreme, the entire system falls apart.

We notice this within alliances that attempt to be an interactive locale intended for the political system in which they are clearly demarcated; barred from inclusivity, whether stranger or friend. We may be surprised if a locale that postures itself as an interaction point of the entire political system is wary of constituents that are part of that system—until we understand that they do not connect to consciousness itself, making every stranger more cognizant of that loss. Whenever a locale is wary of strangers in a manner that correlates with a norm of give and take, or when things do not flow in balanced equilibrium, we can be assured that this locale is a secondary relation.

In fact, we find that a public space or location can quickly switch from being in direct relation to being in a secondary position simply by processing constituents that are external to it. We cannot approximate that the locale originates from pure consciousness—to allow for reflection on interactivity—yet it must be grounded in a constitution that offers social coherence. Paradoxically, the content of this constitution is less important than its role in maintaining interactivity itself. Problems arise when the constitution is overemphasized, mistaking itself for the essence of interactivity rather than its framework. The social broadcasting selection to process external constituents in a more intense manner is not the cause of creating that relationship; rather, it is the very constitution onto which its entrance reflects.

We must ensure that the process of constructing an *interactive embodied environment* is based on a certain contextual layer, despite its prevalence and attempts at universality. However, the context is fabricated as arbitrary and almost unnecessary to the process of the interactive network. It must be contracted simply to give rise to a sentiment that distinguishes itself from consciousness—to allow contemplation of interactivity—so that it must follow a certain constitution that gives it control and regulation over sociality. Yet the constitution is seemingly unnecessary to that contemplation, for it does not really matter which elements are socialized, but rather that interactivity as a process is maintained, regardless of direction.

Often, an *interactive embodied environment* takes its constitution too seriously, as if it were a political or social charter designed to distinguish itself from interactivity, thus becoming a contextually controlled, secondary interactivity.

Usually, the constitution of an *interactive embodied environment* will take some aspect of poignant consciousness or another element relevant to sociality and pinpoint it as its guiding direction. However, if we were to ask the locality whether it genuinely concerns itself with these elements, it would likely admit that it is merely a way of performing a distinguished experience—more related to consciousness than to sociality—and not a means of engaging with those aspects directly.

The same applies to domestication: if we inquire into domestication's constitution of identity, its role in marriage, or any other directive, it would essentially claim that it exists simply as a course that facilitates domestication itself, rather than any of the elements that conventionally define sociality within its bounds. Domestication would prefer to exist in a form that allows interactivity to endure the tests of time, movement, direction, and other forces—and, moreover, to enable interactivity that is not bound by identity or political spectrums. Still, a certain constitution is required for it to define itself and enable domesticity. Often, we find that domestication fails to materialize because individuals are apprehensive about providing a constitution in which they are not even considered interactive bodies.

It is, of course, easy for the constitution to become a fundamental aspect of domestication, such that interactivity is determined solely by that contextual layer—disconnected from consciousness, which becomes a secondary association. This is why we might sympathize with those who strive to adhere to a constitution, believing it will grant their interactivity a universal character, even though this universality cannot exist without domestication. This is not to suggest that constitutions, identities, and domesticated bodies are without further relevance—only that each requires a specific aspect to initiate the process of domestication.

In a secondary interactive structure, operating under the rubric of an *interactive embodied environment*, a natural hostility can arise. These structures are divorced from consciousness, and their interactive experiences do not emerge from conscious material—instead, they are emulations that hover above and are not existentially or fundamentally real to the process of living. Recognizing that element—that it is the very structure they are under which causes that oscillation, rather than a disruption of integration with conscious material—leaves no choice but to find resentment in the entire system. Ironically, sometimes these secondary interactive environments posture themselves as political realms and do so with resounding resentment toward the very political system.

Every political system is already a sort of interactive locale, and so it becomes problematic to interact with that system, as it will automatically become a secondary relation and be disrupted from the flow of consciousness. Therefore, political is both consecrated and untouchable; it is most important but easily disruptive when engaged in any regard. This is why the construction of any interactive locale cannot be politically related and must, in some sense, be distinguished from the political entity.

Moreover, any interactive structure—regardless of its constitution, direction, or construction—can fall into a secondary state by default due to political movement. An interactive locale may lie dormant, providing its provisions in accordance with true consciousness, but due to political attention, it detaches from consciousness, causing the entire interactive locale to become disconnected. This creates a paradox of nature: even if everything is set within a domain to provide ample provisions that allow for attachment to consciousness and domestication for interactivity, it remains vulnerable to surveillance by the political attention sphere or other public spheres. This disrupts its structure and does not enable true interactivity.

This is the case, for instance, when domestication or a similar structure is taken into public interest; the public attention sphere—which coincides with the political—will disallow continuing interactivity. Any attempt to maintain that interactive structure results in its detachment from consciousness, becoming a degeneration of the system, further fostering resentment toward the political system for that provision. In truth, there is no intrinsic tangibility to any domestication, even if assumed to exist, and thus it has no inherent right irrespective of political reality. It is almost as if it is granted amnesty to continue—and when that term expires, domestication is revealed for what it is: a mere measure of political reality, subject to whatever the public sphere deems fit.

It is easy to resent the public sphere for ruining domestication, but if we understand the nature of such repairs, we see that it was a fabrication from the start, as is any interactive locale, and such fabrication is ultimately revealed through the lens of public attention. This is generally not the case in ordinary affairs. Once political attention is present, the interactive locale must degenerate and become a representation within the public sphere, akin to domestication.

It is a burdensome task for an interactive locale accustomed to its interactivity to then dismantle its structure to accommodate what garners political attention. Once political reality disrupts that interactivity, the locale must either entertain that representation and follow its requisites or remain an interactive structure, thereby losing attachment to consciousness. In choosing to follow, domestication is lost, as the locale continues to participate with political attention and diverges from its natural orientation.

Political attention may have little or nothing to do with the locale's immediate conditions; rather, it is simply a matter of perspective, tending toward what it deems fit. Even in an ideal scenario where political attention participates in a certain existential component of the locale, it cannot encompass the entire structure, nor can it persist in that role indefinitely. We expect the locale to evolve, and in doing so, it surely cannot follow a path that perfectly aligns with political attention. This is the difficulty with representations in general: they give the impression of a realistic existential state yet often fail to fully capture it. Even when perfected, a representation remains merely a moment in time—constantly evolving—and thus cannot claim to maintain the existential reality it depicts.

We are now moving away from locales concerned primarily with interactivity and towards those engaged in representation and participation in public affairs. The difficulty for a locale in remaining an interactive structure while participating in the public square is that it is expected to remain interactive rather than devolving into representation. No interactivity remains if it converts as a mere representation; interactivity continues only as long as public attention finds interest in it.

This paradox—afforded by public attention—is destined to collapse. When a structure follows the path of representation, it may continue based on how representations develop and perfect themselves. However, adhering to an interactive structure risks degeneration, as attempts to form interactivity based on representation result only in a performance of interactivity. This does not validate the recurring aspects of the psyche which are separated from consciousness and undergoing domestication; rather, it performs domestication. If the locale recognizes this and sees that it is merely performing interactivity—without any real domestication—it might still continue in its representation without existential disruption, provided it adheres to a representational structure.

When there is a direct conscious connection—a structural connection to a specific locale—even after falling under the rubric of an *interactive embodied environment*, individuals gain their own connection to consciousness and thereby establish themselves as an interactive locale that does not rely on the broader interactive structure of the system. However, the moment they attempt to construct themselves in a strictly contextual direction, their interactivity becomes disconnected from consciousness.

Although permeation does reach the interactive experience, it does so without becoming attached to interactivity. This is because the contextual footprint is such that its full nature does not allow for conscious penetration, yet it should still be regarded as permeating the interactivity nonetheless.

Representations and Interactive Domains

Consciousness, Interactivity, and the Role of the Domestication

An interesting phenomenon befalls when engaging in an interactive domain, which changes and alternates according to the degree of interactivity and embodiment. At the deepest level of interactivity and embodiment, the structure becomes separated from consciousness. Since consciousness is the complete seat of all conceptual structures, there must exist a pathway—an entrance—through which interactivity can introduce any sort of substance. Without such an entrance, interactivity becomes redundant to the point where even the validation of a thought is lost, for the source of consciousness rests with the original proprietor of thought.

Thus, in such locales, the domestication stands in opposition to the structure, providing that necessary entrance to

137

consciousness. Within a highly interactive or embodied environment, the domestication assumes the role of receiving consciousness. This responsibility is imposed upon it because domestication already serves as a receptacle for environments that cannot be separated from conscious influence. In the attempt to integrate the domestication into the domain of interactivity, a disintegration of the domesticative unit often occurs; it loses the objectivity and purpose required to sustain its structure, its only benefit being the continuation of the existing interactivity.

What betterment does the work of domestication offer when the entire sense of interactivity is already supplied by the external environment? Interactivity does not differ among domestication members; rather, changes occur when we enter the realm of consciousness, where each domestication member is meant to serve as a point of biological attachment, thus providing intimacy. In fact, the intimacy gained by a highly interactive structure is the domestication directly conveying consciousness, allowing access to interactive bodies that would otherwise remain unreachable.

Inevitably, a dependency on the domesticative unit arises as it provides the representation and reception of consciousness. In many highly interactive locales with varying degrees of embodiment, the domestication is both praised and placed on a pedestal. It is the substance that allows the entire interactive structure to continue unabated. Consequently, not only does a dependency—and vulnerability to that dependency—arise, but the domestication is also relegated to the background even as its interactivity is presumed to be equivalent to consciousness.

The proponents within the domestication assume this representation, as their receptivity to environments otherwise closed off from the interactive system becomes the means for conscious dissemination. This may appear as a long-term practical solution for a highly interactive domain. Just as the domestication provides interactivity against the central realm of consciousness, in such environments it also offsets the interactivity by offering a representation through which consciousness is distributed.

However, those tasked with structuring this representation and reception are most vulnerable to receptivity—often displaying what might be termed infantile dispositions. Although these dispositions may activate and receive consciousness, they are not fully developed in the sense required to capture its full scope and nuance. In this way, children demonstrate that sweetness is experienced as taste rather than nutrition, a metaphor that holds true for their reception of consciousness. Thus, the reception or dissemination of consciousness occurs in accordance with how children or underdeveloped infantile dispositions perceive it.

Most interactive locales acknowledge this limitation, and thus the task falls to more competent dispositions to elevate the reception of consciousness to a higher degree, providing the necessary nuance. What emerges is a dichotomy in which these dispositions are both venerated and distrusted—they represent the ability of the entire system while simultaneously holding the potential to disintegrate it. There is a paradox: such dispositions are expected to gain competence and receive consciousness in its nuanced form, yet they are relegated to the lowest tiers of the system, preventing them from regulating or disrupting that consciousness even though they hold every key and bolt.

This dynamic explains the general oppression of these dispositions in highly interactive locales. It echoes ancient oppressions—akin to slavery—where subjugated individuals retain potential only to be exploited for consciousness attachment while remaining at the bottom of the hierarchy, thereby being denied the power to regulate or challenge that consciousness.

We can often identify an interactive locale by way of these dispositions and children may be treated with veneration, as they provide access to environments that lie outside the precepts of interactivity.

The Interaction and Embodiment of Psyche in Interactive Domains

The simple interactive or embodied environment is akin to the various elements of the psyche, where each participant—regardless of their perceived importance—manifests with full vitality. In many cases, what might be considered mediocre psyche content struggles to gain traction and is difficult to fortify into a complete picture unless numerous measures are taken. Yet, under the rubric of an *interactive embodied environment*, every aspect of the psyche is expressed fully within the sphere of attention.

Even an infantile memory of insubstantial weight can quickly gain traction, with the *interactive embodied environment* enabling that substance to become the focus of the psyche. In this scenario, an individual might act in an infantile manner even though moments earlier they appeared fully adult-like. This is not a true regression, as there is no sequential consciousness that has led to the accumulation of substantial psyche material; rather, the locale itself allows certain interactive material to gain prominence through the embodiment of sociality, thereby entering the sphere of intention.

Therapeutic and analytical work on the psyche often does not provide adequate mechanisms to negotiate these substances, as every individual retains some irrelevant or underdeveloped psyche content. There are no inherently dysfunctional elements that cause infantile material to dominate; instead, it is the interactive locale that enables this effect. Hence, the therapeutic tradition—in its cool, homeopathic approach to personhood—is deeply relevant in such contexts.

When an interactive substance threatens the stability of the psyche, reintegration with personhood becomes necessary so that this element does not come to define the entirety of the self. In other circumstances, negotiation between conscious elements might allow repressed material to emerge and engage within the attention sphere. However, in the interactive locale, once awareness is achieved, the interaction takes effect immediately, often dominating the individual's personhood unless reconciliation among psyche parts is developed.

This is not to imply that certain psyche elements are inherently deserving or undeserving of integration; one could argue that some aspects should remain as shadows rather than be fully integrated into personhood. Yet, when an interactive substance threatens to monopolize consciousness, the best approach is to integrate it within the wholeness of personhood—reducing it to a subcomponent rather than allowing it to define the self.

Over time, as the psyche fully develops, it becomes evident that the prominence of certain elements is temporary and can be negotiated back to their proper place. Even after reconciliation, continuous negotiation regarding the integration of intellectual material persists. Should a particular voice be activated beyond its deserved level, other psyche elements will counterbalance it, ensuring that any inconsistent motion is mitigated through reconciliation and homeopathic integration. If left unchecked, such a psycho-particle could otherwise threaten to become the entirety of personhood.

Alternatively, some psyche elements may eventually disintegrate from the entire system. In this case, the system itself is recognized as the source of the psyche fragment's ascendancy—it extracts interaction in any direction rather than constituting the wholeness of reality. The individual is not fully integrated with this system, but rather with the wholeness of the self. Once detachment occurs, the compelling nature of the interactive embodiment lessens. Though the interaction remains possible, it no longer poses a threat to the integrity of the person, instead becoming one part among many that warrants attention.

Contextual Oversight and Personhood Development

The definitive direction often taken in such locales is the establishment of a fortified contextual layer, for this ensures there is no fear regarding the aspects involved, as context dictates the entire course of interactions. However, we cannot build or construct a system—or an entire human form—in such a way. What is the purpose of contextual oversight when the interactions it governs do not lead to existential development or progress in meaningful directions for personhood?

Moreover, proper contextual layers are intended to enable or expand interactive material. If functioning correctly, they should elevate into interactive substance that would otherwise not be available. By creating space for new material, these layers make room for certain infantile aspects of the psyche, which may gain influence that is undeserved given their developmental stage. Therefore, there is a need for a homeopathic element to integrate these aspects before they gain prominence and become the defining traits of the individual.

Unfortunately, when this occurs, it only justifies further contextual oversight, disguised as interactive material, which ultimately detracts from the development of personhood. Over time, the entire system and its contextual layers become fashioned by these infantile aspects, which actualize themselves while simultaneously blocking any other interactions that might threaten their established structure. This results in an individual remaining in a childlike state—avoiding growth into a more evolved form, whether it be another aspect of personhood, childhood, or adulthood.

The contextual layer must be constructed through interactive substance, drawing its vitality from what threatens it most. Often, this layer is shaped by consciousness and its reflections, pushing the boundaries of traditional dialogue. However, contextual areas can also be influenced by interactive substance; while they may be distant from universal awareness, they remain integral to consciousness. These areas are personal, wrought by historical precedents and complex communications that ultimately influence their interactive form.

One might question the role of the *interactive embodied environment* within social settings, especially when institutions like domestication, religion, or non-political organizations already facilitate interactivity. The answer lies in the limited interactivity of private units like domestication, reminding us that these forms are trained rather than purely public or political. By altering the *interactive embodied environment*, individual interactivity can permeate all levels of political organization.

The more interactive an organization becomes, the less it depends on traditional leadership. Conversely, in less interactive organizations, strong leadership is necessary to steer the direction. In conceptual overlays, leadership roles are assumed to guide the interactive material. In highly interactive environments—such as cults—leadership may appear arbitrary. Direction flows naturally, even without traditional leadership; the interactive body directs itself according to its needs, simulating leadership without a conventional top-down structure.

As an organization spreads its interactivity across all layers, leadership becomes increasingly necessary. Without a foundational level of interactivity, the organization risks devolving into a random assembly of members rather than a coherent entity. The least interactive organization is typically the political body, as it depends on the amalgamation of various organizations under a political heading, making strong leadership essential to manage the intricate layers and structures within such organizations.

Consider the domestication: it is usually quite interactive and requires significant management and leadership. However, some domesticative bodies—particularly those influenced by identity structures, cult-like dynamics, or other complex systems—do not require strict, militant management. When a domestication is isolated from identity structures or organizations (apart from the political body), its interactivity is often more subtle and nuanced. In such cases, highly ordained direction is necessary. For pastoral or nomadic domesticative bodies that do not participate in social or political organizations, the command of domestication becomes crucial in directing every aspect. In these contexts, low interactivity and high nuance render traditional leadership indispensable. Such a domestication begins to resemble a political system, with layers of representation rather than direct interactivity.

Here, leadership becomes essential to manage the multiplicity of organizational structures.

This leads as expected to the objective of the domestication in relation to the external system in which it participates. In a developed, civilized entity, the domesticative role is to gain advantage and navigate a complex environment. Conversely, in limited or non-civilized contexts—such as nomadic settings—the domestication is relied upon to provide consciousness and its reflective capacity across organizational levels. This mirrors the evolution of civilization, which began with a domesticative role and gradually evolving into structured societies. As civilization develops, the need for nomadism diminishes, as attachment to a complex structure offers greater developmental potential than isolated domesticative bodies.

There is one exception: even within a civilized structure, the domestication may take on a role akin to that of a nomadic entity. It provides a complex, nuanced organization that represents rather than directly interacts. This occurs in the domain of the *interactive embodied environment*. For example, in a cult environment, the domestication may take on the responsibility of offering consciousness that extends beyond the boundaries of the cult. In a dystopian state—where consciousness has been disrupted from the civilized structure—the domestication becomes the entity that organizes consciousness and its representations, even if interactivity is minimal.

In interactive locales, the domestication transforms into a receptor of organizational consciousness and its various representations, rather than just facilitating interactivity. This is especially evident in highly contextualized religious environments, where domestication serves as a bridge to conscious reflection, resulting in decreased interactivity and increased representation of a transcendent element.

Interactive Embodiment and Consciousness Subjection

The *interactive embodied environment* can downgrade because all locales are available for such immediate consequence or notice. When it does downgrade, it does so in a dysfunctional manner. Instead of downgrading to a lesser amount of exposure, the interactive elements lose their embodied stance so that they retain a certain level of embodiment but short for full scope of personhood. This leads to interactions that are inconsistent—not because of some complete psyche element—but rather disturbed psyche elements that are not actualized or materialized in real form.

We could attribute the inconsistent interactions to certain baseline psyche material that has not yet had the opportunity to complete its embodiment. As a result, this material forms a disrupted version of the psyche. In essence, insanity arises when psyche material becomes attracted to certain environmental elements that could offer a full sequence. However, neither the environment nor the psyche produces a definite form. The interactions are inconsistent because the psyche is not fully engaged in the process, and there is no analysis of the scenario contained by the psyche. Furthermore, the environment does not offer a complete response, which means that analyzing the environment in a structural sense yields no clear resolution.

Thus, the answer remains elusive, interactions remain inconsistent, like arrows fired without proper control. Rather than being randomized, these interactions are unconfirmed by evolutionary standards, intellectual material, or environmental structure.

The domain of empire—its interactive locale—represents a mature stage preceding the full flowering of conscious exposure. Like a child whose interactivity is initially unembodied yet potent, there comes a stage when this interactivity becomes embodied, appearing real and authentic. Part of this process is the authentication of experience. Although the embodiment of interactivity may feel genuine, it is ultimately a contextual imagination.

Emotions, sensibilities, and other early experiences accumulate as sedimentary layers of consciousness, rather than being directly linked to it. Consequently, adolescents' often disengage from these early attachments and enter a stage of conscious reception. At this point, they recognize a complex system of interactions that transcends the immediate mirror of experience, aligning themselves with a broader, more intricate system.

This process is analogous to an interactive environment reaching a stage of embodied interactivity, where experiences seem real—at the highest point prior to conscious reception. This stage is necessary for continued interaction within that encapsulation, much like how adults must retain adolescent memories for their continued interaction with society. However, once they reach that delta, they impose a sense of disillusionment on the entire interactive system.

While it is correct to state that interaction is essential for daily conscious reception, it is also true that adulthood becomes a repetitive cycle of adolescent experience. However, adulthood applies maturity in nuanced ways that cannot be reduced to adolescent interactivity. Moreover, consciousness resides above it, making it a temporary domain of interaction with no bearing on settlement or grounding in an existential state or reality.

There are many aspects to notice in an interactive domain to validate its existence. One such aspect is that sociality does not concern itself with the authenticity of that interactivity. As long as it resembles a form of continued conversation, it is enough to sequence those elements within its system. Within conscious subjection, however, there is no such allowance for inauthentic roles. It treats competency above all else.

Interactivity—especially in the body—can reach a phase where there is no need to reach into the abyss of consciousness exposure. Many factors contribute to this, and it cannot be reduced to an adolescent who presumes their experience to be real or who is unwilling to let go of that safety net. The safety of embodied interactivity is very real; they do not experience the shadows or dysfunctions of conscious exposure or subjection. Instead, they continue on the innovative cyclical nature of continuous, perpetual conversations of their choosing. It is like a locale that doesn't truly exist but rather is an imaginative construct.

Because these experiences feel real and somewhat intimate, there is little incentive to reach into a conscious abyss that lacks natural intimacy or deep experiences. Similarly, for adolescents, what would give them reason to transition into maturity, when adulthood seems simplistic, over-generalized, and liken to the commencement of death? While adolescence is filled with vitality, experience, depth, and authenticity, there is little to encourage entering conscious reception.

This situation mirrors being trapped in an organization of imagination. There is little argument to persuade an individual to vacate this imaginative realm because the experiences feel real, the safety is present, and there are no shadows or systemic failures. The only caveat is that it is not real, and its entire direction is based on a tiny dose of conscious sediment that reached into the interactivity; everything that occurs does not matter to the existential state.

Although adolescent memories are personally significant, they are not existentially integral to a nuanced personhood. They are experiments of thought and experience. The moment one departs, it is as though they never existed. In adulthood, every movement pertains to existential regulation, but there is no departure from these thoughts and materials. The only way to leave the imaginative realm is by recognizing it as a mere fabrication and using logical sequences to pinpoint those aspects, until the weary psyche is convinced that it is merely on an imaginative route.

An alternative is to enter into a physical domain of consciousness, which can offer a comparative lens on one's experiences and their *interactive embodied environment*. This approach is risky because one may engage in the universal realm through their perspective of embodied interactivity, without truly participating in that universality. They may dismiss its various movements and instead perceive the event through the lens of adolescence.

Why, then, would one abandon the attachments of interactive embodiment upon entering the physical realm, unless they recognize that what they retain is an imaginative system? Even a prolonged stay in the physical realm may cause an individual to disengage from interactive embodiment. It cannot continue indefinitely to provide the lens through which to perceive reality. Current reality will eventually seep into existential personhood, e.g., the notion of responsibility.

Nonetheless, there is a strong argument for maintaining the *interactive embodied environment* despite its imaginative structure. This locale preserves the critical conceptual framework necessary for interaction within conscious exposure. In fact, it embodies what the psyche must process while engaging with conscious subjection. Therefore, it is essential to retain that locale for the purpose of engagement with conscious exposure.

The same applies to housing or domains: their core function is to provide the structure necessary for the psyche to interact with consciousness. Without such a structure, interaction would not occur; instead, it would simply be an overload of conscious material or basic interaction. We must explore the *interactive embodied environment* to understand how the psyche must be structured when interacting with consciousness.

The immediate response to the imaginative aspects of this realm will be resisted by recognizing their viability and importance within conscious systems. It becomes even more relevant when we note that within encapsulation, there is often a lack of a structured psyche that facilitates proper interactivity. When this is realized, every *interactive embodied environment* gains significance since the locale represents a psyche where no individual is properly interacting contained by a conscious realm.

This makes these locales susceptible to conscious vulnerability, as they represent the noticeable deficiency necessary for its structure. In fact, prolonged conscious reception which does not adhere to the parameters of the *interactive embodied environment* will eventually become diluted and reduced in accordance with its own structure.

It is not enough to simply join the structure of interactivity to the objective conscious insemination; the psyche must also be constructed in a manner that embodies interactivity to continue proper interactions with conscious exposure. If the structure itself is substantial, it is still insufficient; it requires to be the structure of the psyche.

This reflects the famous argument of the adolescents: they notice that adulthood does not retain the embodied interactivity of they experience. As a result, they become disconnected from conscious exposure and lose touch with their perspectives. In fact, the very disruption of conversation between adulthood and adolescence marks the appreciation of adulthood, in its interaction with conscious subjection, all without retaining an invited interactive locale. If they did, adolescents would be a very interesting subject for maturity's disposal, as that is the structure and parameters of engagement within their daily activities.

When an *interactive embodied environment* refuses to separate from its structure and reach into the abyss of conscious possibility, it becomes stagnant and trapped in imaginative cycles. The primary reason for its unwillingness to depart is the belief that the perceived experience is real, especially if anecdotal evidence supports this. Consciousness illumination is a container of an already retained *interactive embodied environment*. Therefore, when we observe conscious subjection, particularly at its center, we recognize that its history has been shaped by an interactive invited locale.

Retaining these elements of embodied interactivity, even though at times it reverts to that stage, the locale encompasses all of them. Unlike an adult who retains the embodied interactivity of adolescence only by memory, but not through structural attachment, a structural realm retains both simultaneously. This reliance on the multiplicity of individuals—some representing conscious reception and others engaging in interactive embodiment—creates a complete and coherent structure.

However, the *interactive embodied environment*, or elements of it, also serves as representations of the infantile aspects or "shadows" of conscious exposure. The structural design depends on both elements: in reality, it is all conscious subjection, and the *interactive embodied environment* is merely a representation. Shadows are the lower echelons of the consciousness hierarchy, representing the infantile stages that eventually aspire to upgrade to full conscious receptivity.

This is their structural design. They also retain the invited interactive element to facilitate recognition of their importance within the system. However, once conscious subjection takes over, it permeates every arena and crevice, making real-time interactive embodiment unavailable. While they may appear to interact, these interactions are structured and embodied, but they are not truly interactive; they are the dissemination of shadow-like material from conscious exposure.

This paradoxical reality—the "shadow" of consciousness—requires both attention to the consciousness sequence and representation of interactive embodiment, though it does not engage in real interaction outside the system. This is a differentiation, but it is not an absolute differentiation, as the conscious system mirrors the individual psyche realm.

In this system, adolescent memories are merely memories, representing themselves to adulthood as temporary domains for proper interaction. They are not existentially or structurally attached. Similarly, in conscious exposure, the interactive embodied elements are not structurally attached but are merely representations that gain traction to continue conscious exposure.

Does a locale set up as an *interactive embodied environment*—under the rubric of conscious subjection—automatically become the shadow of consciousness, whether structured well or not? By choosing to represent the vulnerability of consciousness, it becomes that vulnerability and shadow. Those wishing to retain their *interactive embodied environment*, such as in religion or other system, will benefit by first attaching to the system and retaining the locale's secondary nature, just as adults retain adolescent memories as secondary to their structural design.

True embodied interactivity is essential within a consciousness system, but it is only fully experienced outside its political realm and influence. The further one moves from that realm, the more available they become for genuine interactivity. Upon return, they retain the full dosage of experience necessary to construct the temporary domain for interaction with consciousness. An individual within conscious receptivity cannot retain the experience itself. They are likely to hover over many systems but will not fully embody the existential understanding and experience of each system.

The only way forward is to depart from the locale and physical stature, entering the interactive environment to experience the imaginative realm that allows for deeper interactions with consciousness. The goal of these experiences within *interactive embodied environment*s is to prepare for participation in conscious reception again, without the limitations imposed by the vulnerability of not understanding or retaining a domain of interaction.

The psyche can only sustain the construct of the interactive environment within conscious exposure for so long before its structure begins to degrade, losing its domain-like status. This is why, at the center of conscious propagation, there is an attempted downgrade of its structure, such as weekends, summers, and seasons. These are necessary structures in which the conscious expanse wants to downgrade, as it knows that prolonged periods without an interactive environment will cause the psyche elements to degrade, making them less available for proper interactions.

These downgrades would not be necessary if the system and its individuals understood such, structurally incorporating them, ensuring for reintegration. The system downgrades itself due to individuals' unwillingness to depart.

We often overestimate the psyche's ability to function within both environments. Without the indispensable temporary domains and its memory structure, the psyche will degrade, becoming susceptible to consciousness and its environments. There is no capacity in the psyche to retain a prolonged experience of consciousness without the degradation of *interactive embodied environments*, where infantile perspectives are vital for interacting with maturity.

The same is true for adulthood, in which having children is a crucial ordeal to provide interactive embodiment, granting them access to this realm while remaining in conscious receptivity. However, it is imperative to maintain a clear delineation between external domains and the interactive environments specific to children and adults; conflating these distinct spheres compromises the efficacy of each.

Adults must always retain the experience of infantile stages in real life, in real-time, and through their structural aspects. The domestication provides the necessary provision external to conscious exposure. Those without the domestication become adult-like but lose the necessary infantile locales for proper interaction. In fact, individuals without familial and infantile attachments are likely to be lost to consciousness, due to the psyche's need to retain embodied interactive elements.

The remaining question concerns the stage at which domestication should emerge in relation to conscious vulnerability during maturity. An adult disposition may necessitate essential attachments that exist independently of the structures provided by domestication. Nonetheless, this developmental stage is critical, as domestication must assume a prominent role in shaping the interactive capacities of the adult-like individual. When the time arrives for the enactment of embodied interactivity, it will, by that point, be fully integrated and expressed through the individual.

Adopting a child in their adolescents would involve contracting a domestication that provides the necessary proficiency of embodied interactivity at its purposeful stage. However, it would not be fully embodied, as the attachment to the individual has not integrated into the emphasized stages of personhood. Raising a child from a premature stage allows for the development of their personal stages and growth. By the time they reach the stages necessary for interactive embodiment to facilitate continued adult receptivity, they will be fairly embodied.

Even when a biological connection to an adolescent is established and they are subsequently placed under custodial care, the embodiment of relational depth may remain insufficient. Biological relatedness alone does not guarantee the development of interactivity; rather, it is the sustained, engagement that nurtures such relational depth. As previously noted, the interactive domain is not predicated on notions of authenticity, but on the continuity of interaction itself. In the absence of this cyclical and ongoing dynamic, the adolescent's status is deprived of the essential provisions required for developmental stability.

Representations of the Domestication [Interactive Locale]

The Perplexing Relationship between Consciousness, Interactive Embodiment, and the Domestication

We face a perplexing issue within an *interactive embodied environment*. When the psyche is regulated solely by conscious material and the interactivity inherent in embodiment, it risks entering a cycle of overstimulation. However, the domestication offers a representation that avoids negatively affecting the psyche. To understand this, we must recognize the strain the psyche experiences when combining both consciousness and interactive embodiment. Since interactive embodiment governs the psyche's wholeness (at least for its interactive elements), consciousness provides an enduring framework of reality. When these forces combine, psychic material can become overstimulated. Nonetheless, this dynamic changes within the domestication, which is already a potent interactive embodied system. Its inherent interactivity immediately regulates consciousness—emanating from its representations through an established substructure.

This is comparable to a developed interactive domain where, amid constant receptivity, an interactive buffer allows such exposure to persist. Once the interactive domain loses traction, however, the subjection becomes mere interactivity—detached from the sustaining reality of consciousness.

This protective adjustment prevents overwhelming the psyche with subjection, resulting in downgraded interactivity that does not offer the same benefit to the *interactive embodied environment*. If conscious exposure exceeds its capacity, it will continue at the same pace, eventually overwhelming both the psyche and the interactive framework. Thus, we are left perplexed by the inability to consciously engage within the interactive space—particularly when certain activities lead to a loss of consciousness. This results in a sense of emptiness, as if in a zero-sum scenario. Yet, directly seeking a conscious attachment would destabilize the psyche. Instead, the familial bond provides a conscious connection without triggering constant interactive overload.

The Domestication as a Buffer for Consciousness

Consider an example where the domestication represents a distinct conscious substance. Why does its emanation through the *interactive embodied environment* not overload the system? The domestication is unique within this *locale*; it warrants its own substrate for interaction in addition to embodied downloading. Corresponding to a corporation in an *interactive locale* (especially one that is corporeally represented), the domestication becomes distinct from the interactive environment and links with conscious exposure. Similarly, a well-developed educational institution may not offer interactivity but instead adheres to an external reality or memory of consciousness.

Certain institutions function like embassies for conscious exposure within their embodied environment. These institutions are associated with conscious propagation rather than an immediate interactive atmosphere. An embassy, though part of the *interactive embodied environment*, provides nuanced conscious sentiment due to its attachment to international affairs beyond local interactivity.

Similarly, the domestication is treated as an international system. It is recognized not by its local environment but as an emblem of the individual's biological, psychological, or other structures—regardless of local constraints. Standard relationships based solely on environmental details cannot achieve this effect. The domestication distinguishes itself by being rooted in factors beyond localized parameters, much like an embassy recognized as existing beyond its immediate structure.

These locales can transform into embassies of consciousness within an interactive environment. Not all educational institutions are granted this status—only those that permeate and extend beyond surface boundaries, securing connections with a transcendent sociality. A competent corporation leverages an international sociality emerging from global affairs, thus providing a form of conscious exposure that transcends local interactivity.

A trend emerges: while interactive embodiment is enclosed and potent, meeting certain parameters can yield a locale that immediately connects with conscious exposure. As interactivity is inherently social, when sociality diminishes, the locale shifts to function primarily as an entity of conscious reception. Although conscious exposure permeates all affairs, the interactive locale—restricted by social constraints—limits this potential.

We may then question whether the domestication can exist as an environmental element like local relationships. However, this question leads us into the debate about whether the biological state of a being is truly attached to its environment. When an individual recognizes their biological adherence as international or transcendent, the domestication always retains its status as a nexus of local conscious reception. In contrast, domesticative bodies not based on an immediate interactive structure (such as those influenced by childhood or historical precedence) do not offer the same international advantages. Just as regular relationships focus on the environment, extended domesticative bodies do not pertain to the individual's biological experience at that level, thus not granting that amenity. Intimacy is required for the domestication to serve as an international embassy for the *interactive embodied environment*.

We understand the *embassy* parameters in two directions. One involves a level of intimacy that meets biological standards and extends into the individual's international affairs—reaching beyond the interactive locale. In this state, the individual is receptive not only to interactivity but also to all forms of conscious relationships, even if they remain within the interactive realm. Thus, when intimacy is pervasive, individuals become local nexuses of conscious reception. Not every domestication meets this standard; if based on non-intimate criteria, its members become mere constituents of the environment. However, when it comes to bearing children, the domestication inevitably embodies the complete individual, reflecting a biological encapsulation that grants it international status —or at least political significance.

The second direction involves specific locales within the interactive realm that recognize the subjection of consciousness in all their dealings. Such locales are acknowledged by conscious propagation as a standard of that very encapsulation. To cross the borders of the *interactive embodied environment*, a locale must retain a sociality that consistently interacts with consciousness, ensuring it remains outside of privatization. Not only must sociality enable crossing those borders, but there must also be recognition from consciousness and its various locales of relevant material for encapsulation. This is a tricky parameter; while the entire *interactive embodied environment* may be somewhat relevant to conscious encapsulation (as when it is recognized on a map as part of international standards), the locale itself must supersede its localized environment so that it does not adhere to the same standards—processing its structure instead as an element of conscious encapsulation.

For example, consider the corporation. It is necessary that conscious exposure recognizes the corporation as part of its entity—if the corporation is of any competent stature, it will be integrated into that structure. More importantly, the corporation's structure must adhere to standards that affirm its recognition of conscious sentiment. An embassy may be recognized as an international account for consummation, yet it will not function as conscious subjection if it localizes itself and fails to maintain a sociality beyond its immediate parameters. This requires a highly complex form of sociality that connects to consciousness and, as such, will fail in many locales. Educational and corporate institutions are at the forefront of this competent sociality, as their daily exchanges are based on what might be called the constitution of conscious subjection—providing a structure that separates them from their localized environment.

The Shadow of Political Systems

Even an embassy does not engage in daily interactions that fully adhere to the constitution of subjection; rather, it provides a substandard sociology that does not capture consciousness entirely. It may offer an element of conscious subjection but will not be considered a locale directly linked to it—unless there is a highly developed sociality related to international affairs that causes localized elements to fade away, which is typically not the case.

International brands that enter interactive locales are typically unable to sustain conscious subjection; instead, they become highly prized interactive structures that reflect their immediate environment. In their attempt to stand out and provide that coveted conscious subjection, they often end up offering a more interactive experience that remains heavily attached to their environment. Even if a locale is highly politicized or recognized for international relevance, without a daily sociality that facilitates interactivity and exchange based on conscious subjection, the locale will merely be an impressive interactive embodiment. Examples include certain developed educational institutions and confident corporations—though listing specific examples may quickly become outdated.

Highly prized art installations, architectural feats, and other landmarks typically provide a robust interactive embodiment but are strongly distinguished from conscious subjection. Because these landmarks are environmentally constrained, it is difficult to construct a sociality that reaches beyond their borders. We must remain vigilant in noting that while these locales are prominent in interactive embodiment, they are not to be considered sites of conscious subjection—the key distinction being that conscious subjection is not experienced through their sensory and relational forms.

There is another category that transcends the boundaries of the *interactive embodied environment*: the shadow of the political system. This is not an anomaly. Even a political establishment within the *interactive embodied environment* does not automatically gain access to conscious subjection because it lacks the required parameters. However, if a locale maintains a sociality through engagement with the political system's shadow, it can sustain subjection within the embodied interactive realm.

This occurs because such a locale upholds the parameters mentioned above, retaining a sociality that exchanges material pertinent to the political system—even if it is only the shadow of that system. If a political institution facilitates an exchange of material related to the political system, it participates in conscious subjection. Typically, once a political system is established, there is little incentive to develop a sociality that interacts with additional elements, as the system itself is already set. Still, the shadow continues its subjection, and individuals or groups may gain an embassy-like status, remaining attached to conscious subjection by providing a socially relevant connection.

It is easy to live on a grievance and engage in exchanges centered on that grievance, with the incentive of gaining conscious subjection. However, sustaining such sociality is difficult because subjection is inherently unstable and in constant motion. Many factors discourage this approach. For example, while an educational institution may be a forthright locale that seeks to provide conscious propagation, dwelling on grievances and cultivating a traditional realm of grievances in response to the shadow inevitably produces resentment—since there is always some resentment in the existential state of personhood. Thus, these exchanges continue to participate in the overall consciousness, even as they echo the shadow of the system.

In some sense, it is preferable to remain in the shadow and connected to conscious subjection than to risk losing conscious engagement entirely within the regular realm of the interactive embodied system.

The Actualization of Personhood and Its Challenges

An actualized domain—where one conforms to a former frame of reference to embody a certain sensibility and provide an interactive edge—manifests in a completely different manner. This manifestation is significant because it depends on various interactive components that separate it from the sequential amelioration of personal development, thereby creating a subculture within the preliminary stage of personhood. This domain is problematic when actualized, for it represents a space that once was and now protrudes into the present. Thus, the exchanges must not meet the criteria by which actualization provides interactivity that improperly regulates and controls personhood, bypassing the sequential amelioration of interactivity up to the present moment.

When preliminary frames become actualized, it is incumbent upon the individual to immediately adjust those interactivities in respect to complete personhood rather than merely regulating and moving forward. Failure to do so results in the early stages of an innovative individual governed by an outdated preliminary stage of interactivity.

In essence, unless all interactive edges are inclusively re-integrated, a sequential pattern may re-emerge. If this integration does not occur promptly, every prolonged minute deepens the malformation as the old/new stage of interactivity gains a foothold, strengthening its presence in the present moment.

Studies may even reveal that individuals often base much of their adulthood on an instant where a particular interactivity gained prominence, becoming the defining principle of their personhood. This is disquieting, for it suggests that a preliminary part of the self—one that was not meant to regulate personhood in the present—has taken hold. Worse, there is no availability of change once a previous moment starts regulating the present. Not only is the present lost in the sense that whatever part of the past, by the preliminary stage, is forgotten so that it becomes actualized, but also the fact that because it is not a present interactivity, it becomes cyclical. As a result, it is lost to both its potential and its lineage.

Perceptibly, only a preliminary part of them was not deserving of regulating personhood in the present moment. There is no possibility of change once a previous moment starts regulating the present. Not only is the present lost because parts of the past, via the preliminary stage, are forgotten and actualized, but the interactive edge becomes cyclical, making it lost both to its potential and lineage.

This process operates over extended periods only when interactivity gains prominence due to significant concerns of personhood, retaining vitality throughout the experience. Often, the most repressed or troublesome aspects of personhood—when they emerge prominently—are mistakenly taken to represent the current self. Additionally, these aspects maintain vitality by remaining connected to preliminary stages of personhood. We may refer to this phenomenon as the "amelioration of prior interactivity," which then actualizes as therapeutic mending.

Here, therapeutic properties extend beyond mere healing; they involve the mending of interactivity so that a wholesome, continuous personhood can emerge—one capable of sequential decision-making and realization. However, therapeutic mending can be nearly futile if applied to aspects of the self that are redundant or unworthy of repair.

The Role of the Domestication as an Interactive embodied environment

The same principle applies when the interactive domain is inverted into the domesticative structure, especially when it exists within a locale—subject to conscious subjection. Any domestication outside such an *interactive embodied environment*—whether political, social, or otherwise, such as a cult—would be regulated by external parameters. In this case, the domestication becomes the *interactive embodied environment*, responding to external exposure. What external domains lack is the embodied interactivity that the domestication assumes as its responsibility.

On a more universal scale, any conscious exposure with a domain-ingress is perceived as an interactive experience, not merely a supplement to that subjection. The very act of placing a locale to receive that subjection makes it interactive, rather than directly consciousness-based. The only exception, which forms the premise of this thesis, is within an *interactive embodied environment* external to the domestication. For this domestication, there is no response of interactivity because that would be redundant to the external exposure. Why would they attempt to isolate a point of interaction if that process is already occurring in the public or external sphere? Instead, the domestication takes on a very unique and particular role, acting as the conscious-subjection-embassy to present a representation of what is external to that external domain. It responds to the necessity of the individual, providing a bandwidth of exposure to help retain the semblance of normality within the embodied interactive domain.

Under normal circumstances of conscious exposure, domestication stands in as the provider of the *interactive embodied environment*. What allows it to be centered as embodied is that the interactions relate to biological connections, whether through shared biological experiences or genealogy. Since the domestication does not possess political validation, it can easily be downgraded to a locale of insignificant interactions which are not embodied. However, this would neglect the biological connections, which inherently make them embodied, or avoid them altogether. The interactive aspect manifests naturally because the locale retains all the daily, nuanced informational exchanges that determine its identity.

Instead of considering the domestic locale as a single unit of interactive embodiment, we can explore both the level of interaction and the degree of embodiment. To establish a degree of embodiment, the interactions must maintain a sociality that makes them the "political" experience of the situation. Even though the domestication is not a political reference, within the framework of its locale, there are sub-locales that can be political in nature. These are areas where interactions are the most significant and permeable for all members, contrasted with less political sub-locales, where interactions, though similar, are not as permeable.

An example would be an unclothed child upon a dining table versus within the bedroom, noting the political reference of the dining table and the veneration it invokes. This distinction applies to the degree of embodiment, while the level of interaction depends on the content and context of the interacting members. High levels of interaction occur in situations that are significant to the individual, providing material that presupposes interaction. Low levels of interaction, on the other hand, involve non-stimulating material, which does not hold contextual interest or serve as interactive mirrors within the psyche.

Every psyche already contains interactive substances, perpetuated by external circumstances. Mirroring significant interactive charges is considered high-level because they represent non-processed material, all ready for actualization at any moment. Despite being dormant, they will be mirrored and actualized because they were never given the attention or time they needed in the conscious system of the psyche.

If we consider an individual who has allowed the mesh of interactive particles from their history to accumulate, we would find that there is no potential for high-level interaction. For example, a high-level interaction might occur when meeting a political or public figure because it mirrors a substantial aspect based on a reality framework invoked in that setting. However, if the psyche has already interacted with that reality framework sufficiently, the substantiated interaction would no longer mirror an untapped reservoir, and the interaction would not be considered high-level. This would be difficult with a political figure because it would imply that the individual has already interacted with the political substructure to the point that this new interaction would not add anything further to the premise. A low-level interaction is one that has either already been experienced or does not invoke a framework that has been integrated henceforth.

The Significance of Political and Interactive Aspects within the Domestic locale

The most political aspect of a domestic locale is going to be the centerpiece for its profoundest degree of interaction but not necessarily regulate the interaction itself. Defining high-interactive material is a case-by-case scenario, and it is sometimes the least political aspects that exhibit the highest levels of interactivity. For instance, while the dining area may be the most political, the bedroom may be the most interactive.

We may find that the very act of embodiment can lead to a distilled or disruptive form of interactivity. Since interactivity is a natural result of being embodied, individuals often become protective or cautious about the level and degree of interaction possible. This is why one may be more mannered in the most political aspects but less so in the more interactive ones.

The ability to engage in a multiplicity of interactions is rooted in the lessons of embodiment itself. What is not political cannot be embodied, as there is no convergence between the locale and its various aspects. The lack of convergence disrupts the actualization of the locale as a substance of orientation and instead allows for specific interactivity to take effect.

Although sexual intercourse can be considered a form of embodiment, it may be recognized more as a high level of interactivity unless there is a participation of consciousness between individuals. One may engage in certain political arenas where external propagation is present, which may make them more open to interactive material during the state of intercourse. However, the nature of intercourse is interactive rather than embodied.

For something to become embodied, it requires a sociality that converges in a manner that is external to the privatization typically in effect. This makes the most political aspect of the domestic locale relevant in defining that locale, even if it is not political in the traditional sense. It is political in the sense of convergence and recognition as the centerpiece, though it may not fully reach its political potential.

Anything that is privatized—especially when considered privatized within the locale in respect to the entire locale—exists somewhat within the parameters of privacy. However, if it is privatized within that locale and within its specific context, it will lack the political aspect and convergence necessary for these sub-locales to be considered interactive or embodied.

When no interactivity is available, it becomes delineated from the locale and excluded from its parameters. Interactivity is only gained by being attached to the subjection of the locale, which emanates from the centerpiece or most political aspects of its structure. While the propagation is based on individuals and their interactions with externality, the structural manifestation of this subjection is what matters. Therefore, in accordance with the interactivity of its sub-locales, the consideration of the structural centerpiece will finalize the actualization of the locale.

It is important to note the differentiation between sub-locales that are structurally disconnected from the political centerpiece. Despite the ownership or framework of different locales and their single sentiment, they still lack interactivity due to their structural detachment. These sub-locales can be viewed almost as the "shadow" of the house—such as the barn, backyard, or guest house. Any interactivity within these subdomains will not be considered in relation to the domestic locale but rather as something separate, often viewed as a shadow or a space one either runs from or towards.

The Role of Therapeutic Properties in Integrative Healing

Therapeutic mending is purposeful only when there are conflicting interactive pockets that require wholesome sequential pattern to resolve. Habitually, it is employed to create a composite picture that goes beyond the interactivity currently in prominence. Therapeutic mending becomes possible when one presumes that only a specific, partial aspect of their personhood requires repair—while the growing sensibility of external interactivity is repressed. Ironically, this process can disrupt its very purpose: to establish a sequential pattern for a wholesome self. Instead, it may lead to the mending of isolated portions of personhood, allowing one to gain prominence in certain domestic conflicts while major conflicts remain unaddressed.

We might then question the contemporary necessity of therapeutic cleansing as distinguished from its past forms. In modern periods, the number and size of interactive domains have grown so significantly that what was once a momentary aspect of life has become a daily necessity. In previous eras, therapeutic mending was a natural process, for which the psyche recognized differentiations between interactivity, beginning the process of unity and amelioration.

However, we could also have the prerogative for which the previous eras did not have the availability of assorting conflicting interactive domains, so the natural process was allowed and endeavored without the costly effects of existential change. When interactive pockets are outsized, the existential department of the psyche will engage with each and every one, making mending more complicated.

In this modern context, the individual is akin to an embodied empire, where the unity of its subjects —and their differentiated aspects—demands a more intricate approach to mending.

In earlier times, leadership in smaller domains did not require continuous mending because fewer complex parts demanded attention. In contrast, modern smaller organizations may require more frequent shifts in approach to prevent stagnation, balancing simplicity with complexity.

A king does not possess the amenity to proclaim the unity of all parts—such an act would generalize what is specific and dilute its complexity. In contrast, one who masters a smaller domain, as seen in earlier eras of the individual psyche's exposure, finds mending simpler because the complex parts are fewer. Moreover, tending to a larger kingdom requires a constant process of mending due to its increased complexity and differentiation; here, mending is one of the primary requirements of leadership. The system and its constitution already proclaim themselves through its complex parts and differentiation of systems, positioning leadership to pivot away from the natural sequence. However, if leadership pivots too extremely, complexity is reduced to simplicity and differentiation is lost, thereby diminishing the kingdom's essence.

Conversely, one who manages a smaller sphere experiences less necessity for perpetual mending because there are fewer complex parts demanding constant unity. In fact, leadership in smaller organizations may even need to depart from the natural sequence of simplicity to cultivate a more complex structure. In such cases, the natural cause and effect is the mending of parts—mirrored in one another—unless an obstruction prevents them from coinciding and ameliorating in likeness.

The therapeutic properties we discuss here do not require further detailed explanation. It is sufficient to say that a therapeutic process should enable the embodiment to integrate all interactivity rather than focus narrowly on its individual parts.

In some cases, the worst outcome of a therapeutic process is dialogue that directs the interactive course in a manner that fails to yield a wholesome picture of personhood. Instead, therapeutic mending should allow external and internal connections to coalesce, balancing all aspects of interactivity without overemphasizing or subduing any single element. Although certain artistic expressions may bolster this integrative effect, they can sometimes be counterproductive if misapplied—emphasizing or dampening particular interactive parts, or gaining prominence only through conceptual interaction rather than genuine emotional stimulation.

Certain domains—especially those marked by resentment—always reflect a preliminary stage of one's wholesome personhood. Resentment or hostility often signals that a part of the substructure is threatening to become an unbalanced interactive edge. This reaction is a fear that the preliminary interactive stage might gain undue prominence and begin to regulate personhood. However, it is important that an individual experiencing such hostility does not estrange themselves from this material.

Once resentment arises, it tends to gain prominence despite any resistance from the overall sense of personhood. The visual complexity and vastness of interactive pockets mean that dormant aspects often manifest based on external experiences. Whether it is hostility, anxiety, or another emotion, the next step is to incorporate these preliminary interactive edges into the wholesome interactive self. Rather than using the psyche's energy to combat the notion of hostility, it is more constructive for the individual to reconcile with the interactive component that has emerged from external experience.

In the process of mending these interactive parts, one becomes aware of potential changes in voice and existential makeup. Although these parts are preliminary relative to the current personhood, they remain necessary for future development. To progress, one must acknowledge that the present structure is neither perfect nor fully developed—it awaits interactive aspects and voices that deserve inclusion. This requires current feelings to honor prior structures, even if they conflict with present sociality. The individual is formed by current interactive assumptions, with a sociality that both mirrors and provides nuanced realization.

When faced with preliminary interactive edges and the manifestation of external experiences, the wholesome nature of the present structure and its encompassing sociality is threatened. Although change in sociality must accompany personal change, the preliminary interactive aspect is but a small voice in the broader, complex development of personhood. Nonetheless, there are times when this preliminary stage is so significant that its integration restructures the current system. If one remains true to the lineage and developmental process, allowing these preliminary voices to gain prominence will not adversely affect the whole system; rather, their allegiance is to the overall system, not merely to a specific moment.

A concrete example, and one likely to remain prevalent, is the case of religion. Secular-minded and universal individuals may feel resentment toward the interactivity inherent in religious aspects. This resentment stems from the preliminary stages of their own development, as all religions are founded on specific interactive domains that contribute to individual development. Although religion is not a direct manifestation of interactive material, for universally minded people it represents highly contextualized domains inherent in the substructure of any system's evolution.

For the universally minded individual, religion often connects to infantile stages—particularly childhood. Resentment toward religion, then, signifies an unwillingness to address these early stages of development. The sequential nature of the psyche processes information much like the developmental stages of religion, a process recognized immediately despite the distinct character of religious practice. Conversely, resentment can also emerge from religion and onwards toward universally minded aspects. In such cases, religion represents a lack of reality in the system's substructure—a reminder of a more wholesome nature lurking beyond, highlighting the fallacy of certain premises. Through therapeutic mending, the religious individual may eventually become more universally minded, though the cycle of resentment may then require further therapeutic intervention to mend the adversary inherent in religious representation of one's infantile nature.

Contextual Frameworks and Regulation of Interaction within the Domestic locale

Similar to a contextual overlay within an interactive embodied domain, the domestic locale goes beyond merely providing an interactive embodiment—it offers more than just the passing influence of the wind.

It becomes a specific criterion of interaction, shaped by particular assumptions about how that interaction should unfold. For example, in a domestic unit that is highly religious or follows another specific framework, individuals will not interact based on universal sentiment but rather according to the criteria of that framework. This contextual regulation directs the interactions; although they are considered embodied, they are influenced by a direction removed from any direct relationship with universality, which remains dormant outside their domain.

The domestic locale exists within a domain that interacts with universal manifestation, but only within its own limits. This provides an easier pathway, as the contextual domain naturally regulates the system by offering a controlled framework for interaction. Without such contextual overlay, individuals might fall into mirrored interactions that lack foundational purpose—reflecting arbitrary processes that do not support actualization. This is a common issue as a result of *interactive embodied environments*, where embodiment can process any or all interactions regardless of the structured individual and their nuanced needs.

One might argue that mirrored interaction is necessary for instantiation since the stimulation itself validates the interaction. However, actualizing specific, isolated aspects of personhood does not benefit the whole person, but only that specific aspect. This type of actualization may even be regressive, causing the individual to revert to infantile patterns that undermine the productivity of a more developed interactive experience.

To prevent this, a religious framework or an alternative form of external contextual regulation controls the interaction, ensuring it remains within the parameters of that domain. The context is not personal or based on the individual's particularity; it remains external and prevents the direct mirroring of interactive substance. Even when aspects of the context are relatable, they do not provoke direct mirroring because they remain distant from individual identity.

When the domestic locale functions optimally, it becomes an interactive embodiment that can be engaged at any level without being confined by a rigid contextual framework. Naturally occurring frameworks—such as child-rearing, family dynamics, and other familial concerns—outline the environment, but are flexible enough to avoid imposing rigid structures, thus allowing the locale to remain a wholesome interactive space. When this balance is achieved, individuals must choose the direction of their interactions, as there is always a risk of mirrored interaction. The domestic locale must then be used purposefully to achieve specific objectives aligned with the individual's objectives.

At a political level, one might assume that a broader environment offers supplementary interactive possibilities; however, this superintends the notion that it does not operate like a domestic locale. In the political sphere, despite its broader landscape, individuals cannot occupy society solely based on their peculiar contextual outlook. Such engagement is only possible within the domestic locale.

When individuals attempt to impose their own contextual direction within the political environment, they operate within a subdomain rather than a universal one. As a result, sociality begins to dominate their perception of reality, overshadowing their intended direction. Moreover, political interactions become detached from direct engagement with external reality as social frameworks impose a regulatory subdomain. Within the domestic locale, however, this dynamic shifts. Interactions can be directed toward a contextual objective without creating a subdomain or isolating the interactive space. This is because the domestic locale is defined by its direct social interactivity, where the act of interaction itself becomes the means of achieving direction.

This dynamic can shift into a subdomain when there is a pathological focus upon the specific context, where interactivity takes on a role similar to that of religion—not based on merely propagating towards interactivity. When the domestic locale is anchored in a specific interactive or conflict-related framework, it suffers more than the political locale would. The entire contextual outlook then revolves around them, providing specific interaction within the context of that conflict or pathological interaction. With its embodiment, this would be perceived as a wholesome, absolute reality, fostering an inconsistent mindset that typical conflict could not provoke.

A parallel exists in the political-interactive-embodied environment, which assumes a contextual direction that deems the conflict as true and wholesome, allowing for an embodied interactivity of all the inconsistent mirrorings of conflict-prone aspects in the individual's history. However, under the regulation of its structure, the system mitigates such inconsistencies, preventing the extremes found in the domestic locale. In the domestic locale, the contextual direction directly affects interactive embodiment. Conflict is experienced with full embodiment, and interactivity is mirrored from an inconsistent formation of the individual's history, resulting in a volatile conflict that becomes the only perceived reality as well as the truth of personhood.

There is no mitigation of the contextual attention because it relies on sociality, which is limited by both person and environment. This leaves little room for the dynamic-nuance that would naturally emerge in the political manifestation of such. Instead, individuals become simplified characters in a simplistic dynamic, risking an interactive embodied experience perceived as the wholesome reality of all their interactive layers. A conflict in the external realm of consciousness will not be experienced in the wholeness of their reality framework because interactivity—and especially embodiment—is separate from consciousness. For this reason, prolonged conflict in a conscious based setting, if sustained, becomes an interactive embodiment. Conflict and combat, then, are not occurrences of conscious subjection but rather of embodied interactivity.

Well-established civilizations, therefore, avoid conducting military campaigns within their own territory—at least not from their centers—to prevent interactive embodiment from disrupting the continuous flow of their core cultural receptivity. The domestic locale, by relying on social interactions to define its space rather than structural development, directs those interactions based on interactivity. This flexibility allows for inconsistent contextual changes, while political systems tend to be more inconsistent in their interactions and rigid in their contextual frameworks. The political locale's stubbornness arises from its structural dependence, which solidifies a contextual framework embedded in its system, making it difficult to depart from its sequential output. In contrast, the domestic locale depends on specific interactions, making it challenging to remove them without destabilizing the locality.

This principle is evident in psychological processes: what is difficult to change contextually is often easier to shift interactively, while stagnant interactions facilitate contextual change. For example, a corporation is typically stagnant in its interactions but adaptable in its contextual approach, while a friendship thrives on interaction yet may struggle if its contextual foundation becomes stagnant. The same principle applies to a corporation, which, although reliant on its contextual structure for growth, would collapse without sufficient interactivity. In contrast, if the context itself becomes stagnant, the corporation loses vitality. Similarly, a friendship thrives when both context and interaction remain dynamic and flexible.

When balancing vitality in both context and interaction, challenges arise. A corporation that becomes more interactive may struggle with contextual change. As interactivity increases, the need for a solid contextual foundation grows, creating tension between flexibility and stability. This is most evident in cult-like organizations, which promise high interactivity but become entrenched in an unchanging, nonnegotiable context. An optimal system transitions from a reliance on context to a reliance on interaction, allowing flexibility in both areas. Political systems, for example, maintain a foundational structure—such as a constitution— while permitting dynamic changes within interaction, thus balancing stability and flexibility.

However, when a system emphases too much on a specific interactive aspect, it risks becoming entrenched and prevents further evolution. Non-embodied interactive structures remain flexible by adapting their contextual formation without locking individuals into rigid patterns.

Lastly, problems arise when an embodied locale becomes too tied to a specific contextual overlay that may not align with the individual's needs or reality, leading to a loss of personal autonomy. A healthy interactive system, however, allows the individual to direct the contextual focus, ensuring that both interactivity and context work together to support the whole person.

Additional Reflections on Context and Interaction

However, the domestic locale will be inconsistent in its contextual direction because that is not the dependency of the system. It can find a new contextual direction in a moment's lapse—the change of interactivity. Although we have noted that individuals are unwilling to negotiate the interaction themselves, the depth of an interaction means that the domestic locale finds it difficult to change contextual direction; this would require a relinquishment of the interactive material in order for a new context-premise to be realized.

This phenomenon is evident in psychological nature: what is contextually difficult to premise tends to be interactively permeable, whereas what is interactively stagnant will be more amenable to contextual change. For instance, a corporation is iteratively stagnant in its interactions and thus more adaptable in changing context, while a friendship is interactively permeable yet stubborn in its contextual development.

Because there is only one aspect assumed to be the dependency for the reality structure—an aspect widely acknowledged as troublesome for negotiation—it remains essential to recognize which aspect is dependent in restricting movement within that facet. The other aspect, by its nature of being nondependent for the reality framework, will be more easily negotiable and may even serve as a coinciding premise that demonstrates the system's proper functioning. If both the contextual premise and the interactivity are stagnant, the system will appear stale and lose vitality, threatening the overall reality framework. Any prolonged structure lacking vitalization becomes diminished in its attachment, leaving the remaining aspect as the sole actualization of a living, vitalized locality.

For example, a corporation, though unviable for changes in interaction and dynamic nuance, will depend on its contextual premise for the promise of development through evolving growth despite weakened interactivity. Acknowledging that the corporation depends on interactivity for its system—and that without sociality and an agreement on dynamical terms would become destitute. While at the same token, if it were to be contextually stagnant, it would be noticeable as a non-vitalized system, for the interactivity is already low, and now the context has remained the same.

While on the other side we have the friendship, which relies on its reality structure not on interactivity as is assumed, but the contextual footprint that allowed the friendship to manifest. This is the most contentious of the friendships, for it is this that the entire locale is relied upon. The interactivity can be quite high, without a change in a contextual formation, which would have the system at regular levels. When the friendship loses interactivity, then it loses its viability, for the context is already stagnant, for now the interaction is also on a low, to then become disengageable for continuation.

When both context and interaction are provided with vitality, a new criteria arise. For instance, a cooperative entity that aims to become more interactive may be at a loss for contextual change because both cannot be simultaneously entertained. The more interactive something becomes, the less negotiable the context is. As interactivity takes precedence, the system must cement the reality structure into a fixed formation. It cannot rely solely on interactivity—which is permeable and subject to change—but must appeal to the contextual connection to deepen its roots so that interactivity can flourish.

This is found most egregious in cult formation, which is usually the promise of a high interactivity, to then become so rooted in a specific contextual argument or premise that is unchanging and even unnegotiable. It is the very attempt at providing a continuous promise of interactivity that makes the system rely on a specific contextual anchor for all that change.

Instead, the optimal system moves from context reliance to interactive reliance, so that it can leverage in accordance to provide the nuance change from both sides. But at any moment, there will be an anchor and the provision afforded to that anchor, whatever it may be. We notice competent political systems are usually of this temperament, where it will hinge to a contextual focus, such as its constitutional ground, which will allow a fair amount of interactive change as its provision: to then pivot to a specific interaction which will allow the premise of contextual change to follow a sequential process.

When they are in such a formation, there will arise contentiousness to the interactive aspects which are relied upon and will be repressed for the system to function. While during contextual adherence, contention issues will concern the contextual stance and its nuances.

This leads to the issue of the interactive and embodied environment. Here, the system substantiates itself as interactively formatted, with the only premise being a contextual formation anticipated to supplant it. The locale is not available to ruminate on a specific interactive aspect, as doing so would limit the potential for volatility in contextual interest. In its permeable, far-reaching interactive experience, any attempt to pivot solely to an interactive aspect can entrench the embodiment, restricting one's perception solely to that aspect.

For non-embodied interactive structures, however, the absence of physical embodiment allows the system to follow its interactive aspects and shift its contextual formation without threatening the wholeness of personhood. A further problem arises when the interactive substrate of an *interactive embodied environment* is engendered, for they develop to be anchored to the contextual overlay that allows the whole system to be. This contextual framework does not necessarily reflect the desired course, nor does it fully encapsulate the accurate nature of personhood. The interactive process will, to a significant extent, outline the individual's sense of self, structuring their perception of experience. However, this interactive dynamic remains intricately linked to the contextual foundations upon which it depends, despite the existence of a more expansive and rounded reality which transcends such contextual constraints.

Especially considering that a proper interactive biological system will not be specifically contextualized but rather be available for any and all interaction, so that by following whatever interaction comes forth, it is not the case of following any sort of sequence that is necessary for personhood or reality. Instead, it behooves the individual to provide the contextual direction for the interactivity, for the entire premise of the locale is to provide interactivity and thus marry it to the individual who provides the contextual layer.

The locale doesn't promise to provide context to which the individual brings an interactive system, because any attempt at such would only be the delineation of that system for whatever interaction comes forth, and its inconsistent formation. The same can be said for any locale in which the expectation is of one kind, so that the corporation will expect contextual nuance instead of interactive development, and one who attempts the interactive aspect is going against the premise of the entire locale. It will be as if the individual is manifesting the shadow of the entire system instead of interacting with its potential.

The same can be said for a friendship, in which an attempt to change contextual formation will be at the peril of the entire locale in lieu of what it is meant to provide, which is interactive experience. However, through interactive experience, it does pivot towards a contextual formation, which if one does not agree or does not seek to follow, would be the case of differing friendships.

This is why the corporation is more structured, in that it does not solely undertake an interactive experience—this can be found elsewhere—while its contextual nuance is available in varying degrees so that no one is forced into an unwanted reality. The only disruption arises when interactivity is low, resulting in a lack of vitalization in the system or when the individual relies solely on the system's movement despite contextual stagnation.

Embodiment and Contextual Regulation: A Temporal and Social Dynamic

We may notice a temporal differentiation in the embodied environment—a differentiation not solely dependent on specific social settings but rather exemplified by them. In the morning, due to certain psychological movements (or their absence), embodiment reveals itself, and the locale is downgraded to a more simplistic interactive state. It may seem peculiar to attribute psychological functionality and the premise of embodiment merely to the fact that it is morning. When the contextual domain is most active, there is less room for embodiment because the interaction is more directed. Although the final outcome of an interaction is embodied, the highly contextualized entry funnels its substantiation through a narrow framework, thus diminishing its embodied stature. In other words, the more contextualized an interaction is, the less embodied it becomes; conversely, the more embodied it is, the less it is contextualized.

The challenge arises when seeking complete embodiment, which becomes attainable through a lack of direction—mirroring the most immediate aspects of personhood in an inconsistent fashion. Full-scale embodiment can prove wearisome, as it directs a substance unnecessary for the sequential pattern of individual identity. Conversely, complete contextualization renders interactions into mere imaginative figures that serve the underlying thesis, with no intellectual separation since the premise always precedes the interaction. In this case, the social experience becomes a mere validation of the psyche's proclamations—a simulation that furthers the objective rather than constituting genuine interaction.

The spectrum between contextual overdrive and immersive embodiment represents two extremes that can become wearisome for psychological engagement. This brings us back to the premise: the *interactive embodied environment* is downgraded to a mere interactive state when highly contextualized psychological processes dominate that period of the day. In social settings, this process allows embodiment to regulate easily in the morning—or on holidays and rest days—while the interactive aspect is weakened. In the evening, however, the psychological process loses its grip on contextual formation, and sociality reflects that change, leading to an actualization that becomes an interactive embodiment.

When this occurs, it can be the case that all individuals then immerse in a near complete embodiment without direction or course, thus making for a very inconsistent sociality and experience, or the contextual regulating is maintained, in which the individual still controls and directs the interaction in its due course. However, the contextual requirement, when the sociality is geared towards complete embodiment, is going to need to be a very high degree, for every slip of its regulating leads to a deeper interactive experience.

It might even be beneficial for an individual to be less available for contextual focus in the morning, thus permitting embodiment to occur, with the understanding that later social receptivity will offset that. In the evenings, a higher degree of contextualization is necessary so that embodiment permeates existence without triggering inconsistent psychological functioning. If one seeks interactive embodiment, the highly contextualized morning can offer a buffer for that process—even though any resulting embodiment may prove true only in terms of individuality.

Genuine embodiment requires an environment that fully permeates such sentiment, yet that very environment risks complete embodiment that might undermine the intended process. Furthermore, when sociality reaches a state where it downgrades to inconsistent functionality, even a robust contextual framework may fail to direct the interactive flow, as information travels quickly and any lapse in focus can lead to inconsistent function. Additionally, the psyche's metabolism demands an enormous energy supply to maintain contextualization while embodiment occurs, as it is essentially regulating the entire social landscape for the individual's benefit.

One way to grasp this dynamic is by considering sexual intimacy as a form of embodiment—in the sense that, for a moment, it seems solely focused on interaction. However, if contextual regulation or distraction intervenes, the interaction becomes non-embodied, reducing it to mere functionality. In contrast, an evening scenario might more closely resemble an embodied sexual experience—one free from overbearing contextual regulation or distraction—yielding a wholesome encounter. During intercourse, it becomes exceedingly difficult to shift from a state of pure embodiment into one governed by contextual regulation; the interaction tends to mirror whatever stimuli enters the mind.

In situations of low sexual stimulation, distraction, or alternative focus, sexuality may not be embodied at all, forcing the individual either to redirect their attention to stimulate interaction or to reconcile a conflict between the desire for embodiment and a lack of focus. If intercourse follows a conventional route without embodiment, it may even lead to resentment, as the body is engaged while the desired embodiment is absent. In either extreme, the psyche's drive to achieve embodiment—combined with its sequential regulatory process—results in an experience that inconsistently activates dormant interactive components rather than fostering a wholesome, integrated personhood.

Unlike sexual experience—where exceptions might sometimes be acceptable—there is no bypass for either embodiment or contextual regulation in the broader social realm. The environment is both offered and regulated in accordance with the psyche's needs. Some individuals require a high degree of embodied interaction, though they risk jeopardizing this by engaging in interactions that do not follow a sequential pattern aligned with their identity. Others may choose to avoid the inconsistent nature of full embodiment in favor of strict contextual regulation; however, this choice can come at the expense of genuine interactive authenticity, as interactions become artificially stimulated and fail to accurately reflect external sociality. Abandoning the *interactive embodied environment* altogether means forgoing the benefits of both modes. Instead, one must decide whether to participate in conscious receptivity or to withdraw into a makeshift interactive space—whether embodied or non-embodied.

When engaging in conscious receptivity, a well-constructed contextual domain is essential—not so much to regulate social interaction as to serve as a haven for receiving and distributing conscious information for individual functioning. Without this framework, the interaction with subjection may be mistaken for an embodied environment rather than a deliberate, thoughtful engagement. In the absence of a robust interactive base, the psyche compels the creation of its own contextual framework to facilitate interaction. Much like an *interactive embodied environment* can become inconsistent by selecting any available interactive substance from the psyche, conscious receptivity will latch onto any accessible contextual formation because it cannot simply be ignored or absorbed in its raw form. This inconsistent selection might draw on simplistic, past frameworks, thereby shaping the entire interaction from an infantile perspective. Even when relying on familiar, established frameworks, overly rigid parameters can force encapsulation to enter in a forceful, unruly manner, thereby protecting the contextual framework by validating pre-existing assumptions. In this way, instead of nurturing unaffected interaction, individuals may end up using subjection merely to confirm their existing beliefs. This is why constructing—and deconstructing—contextual domains when engaging with subjection is paramount. Often, individuals unknowingly maintain a highly regulated contextual domain in which the process of subjection is so tightly controlled that little room remains for the subjection's independent influence. Consequently, many who inhabit environments with high degrees of exposure may appear to experience little of it—not because the encapsulation is absent, but because the individual's own regulatory framework dominates the interaction.

The Contextual Domain and Its Challenges

The contextual domain designed to receive and integrate conscious sentiment differs fundamentally from domains serving non-propagating contexts, such as those of pure *interactive* embodiment. Its objectives are twofold: to maintain relatability for the individual and to preserve an unaltered reception of the original encapsulation. Rather than transforming the encapsulation, the domain focuses on its inherent wholesomeness while adapting it for individual needs. This particularization is the hallmark of the contextual domain—it establishes the limitations and relatability parameters for the individual. Participation in exposure is not inherently required, but arises due to individual constraints. Whatever construction enables such particularization remains temporary and unstable as a method of interaction, rather than constituting the interaction itself. Over time, the domain naturally reverts to the themes present in the encapsulation, as the encapsulation itself evolves and develops its own personality. This intrinsic personality may not be fully comprehensible, but it becomes evident through the themes unique to each moment and location. The goal is not to construct the contextual domain for its own sake, but to discern trends within the subjection that allow access to themes beneficial for both the subjection and the individual. In examining the individual, one finds that every element correlates with the encapsulation and its history; all aspects naturally interconnect. The only factor that might disrupt this connection is an adversarial contextual domain that causes disruptive interactions or even transforms the encapsulation into an entirely new form.

A common pitfall in describing these domains is constructing one that is overly restrictive. A contextually narrow domain risks failing to relate to the individual, thereby undermining its purpose. Even if exposure is present, an overbearing domain may prevent the individual from fully engaging with it—a scenario often seen in restrictive frameworks, such as certain religious paradigms that do not align with personal parameters. Another issue is when the domain lacks receptivity to external influences; even if it meets individual needs, it may fail to adequately integrate external information. Since the individual and the exposure are fundamentally intertwined, the domain cannot ignore either. Overcomplicating the domain or repressing certain material can render it unrelatable, obscuring its inherent accessibility. Even if access is disturbed, the domain must remain immediate and serve the individual; if it becomes entirely unrelatable, it will lack the vitality to sustain itself. Access can also be disrupted by inverting the domain's parameters—making every element its opposite—which results in ironic prose that obscures the true intent. Although the psyche is open to refractive and poetic interpretations, excessive reliance on strict irony causes the intended message to be lost, diminishing access even as relatability persists. This challenge is especially evident in political conceptualizations, which are inherently metaphorical. A state is neither an individual nor confined by individual parameters; the only way for an individual to interact with a political formation is to view it as a metaphor for their own life, allowing it to reflect personal systems. However, this often leads the political organization to become overbearing, pushing the metaphor to extremes that, while relatable, reduce access to its intended meaning. As a result, such metaphors may be regarded as genuine even though they function merely as constructs—much like any narrative. In our contemporary era, this process appears particularly ironic given our widespread inability to recognize it.

The Contrast of the Interactive and Centric locale

There is a convergence between the interactive domain and the centric propagation in that both offer nuanced, time-bearing qualities. The interactive domain is a scheduled locale that permits both inconsistent and purposeful engagement with variations not available to a sequential system. For this reason, it is most attainable during the morning function. This is owed to its inherent weakness in embodiment and, regarding interactivity, a lack of depth and quantity. Such characteristics create a contextual overlay that naturally regulates the interactive structure and provides formative direction in the interactivity.

This contrasts with the centric propagation, which is also at a weak point for the embodiment of the system and thus more contextual in its mornings, however, differing in that it is the necessity of that system to enter into a premature state of embodiment, for the context is inhibiting the forthright experience that is due for its potential. We would not give guidance to the interactive locale to embark on more interactivity, for its ideal scenario is the natural manifestation of the morning, and any tinkering, either in extra context or more interactivity, will be a wrongful turn from the ideal. While the centric locale has not manifested the ideal scenario in the morning, because context is only in service of a temporary platform for interaction, not a reclusive standpoint for regulation. As the day progresses, the factors change accordingly for both locales.

In the interactive locale, as the morning context begins to fade, interactivity becomes unhinged from direction and stabilization. Regulation then requires maintaining the context throughout the natural diminishment, even as the momentum of interactivity grows. By evening, interactivity reaches a tipping point, becoming thorough—especially in high social environments—and it may then assume the quality of embodiment rather than inconsistent interactivity.

Although the sensibility of embodiment shares similarities with dynamic interactivity, there are major divisions in their composition. The enlarged interactivity stakes a claim on individuality, rendering the experience fuller, though not necessarily embodied. Instead, the interactivity entertains inconsistent facets of the psyche and is not a direct consequence of the external system. Even when one appears to engage with the external realm through a semblance of embodiment, this engagement is not integrated into the encapsulation.

It is akin to a desert where one projects a certain appearance, with internal happenstance mirroring an external manifestation. Those who have never participated in revelatory higher consciousness might assume this realm lacks any true consciousness or embodiment, perceiving it simply as a desert simulating the centric locale. In stark contrast, the centric locale ensures that any higher life form—despite previous connections to consciousness—will undergo a significant psychological formation through its convergence. This indicates that the centric locale is actively propagating and thus qualifies as an embodiment, while experiences in the interactive locale should be regarded as projections of prior genuine interactions with consciousness.

As the day transitions, the centric locale's contextual regulation begins to fade, paving the way for the ideal scenario. By evening, the embodiment becomes so pronounced that it requires deliberate regulation to maintain proper interaction.

Subjection and Disbursement

The Flow of Consciousness and Its Limitations

We will notice that consciousness propagates from the center is afforded its pathway according to that succession. This would mean that if the center locale does not alleviate its movement and expansion—the resulting properties will remain unchanged. We cannot expect peak consciousness to operate like a continuous flow of electricity, as this would lead to a state that neither supports self-reflection nor accommodates simultaneous processes. Therefore, we do not experience a constant propagation of consciousness from the center, whether throughout the day, week, or momentous occasions. Instead, it uses these changes to alleviate the burden of being in a peak state. Consequently, the center will function as a minimal system, allowing it to process developmental changes.

This same principle applies to individuals: their peak consciousness is not always present or propagating but is rather a fleeting experience when they reach that peak. On a regular basis, individuals remain within the system of the psyche, internalizing the process. By definition, internalization cannot result in complete subjection. Individuals must internalize consciousness; and attempting continuous subjection would lead to stagnation and disruption, transforming the system into one that performs tasks without recognizing its processes. As a result, striving for a continuous peak causes individuals to lose their connection to the necessary lower levels of consciousness, ultimately losing grip on peak consciousness. What we hold most dear is often lost through pure interaction; a certain distance from peak consciousness is necessary for proper engagement. Without this distance, degraded interaction undermines the formation of consciousness and leads to its improper construction.

This principle also applies to structural consciousness. Peak consciousness does not sustain a continuous flow of exposure. Instead, it spends most of its cycle ensuring the stability of systems, reaching its peak only briefly. When not engaged in subjection, each dependent locale misses out the real-time subjection. As the center locale downgrades, so too does the dependent locales. This dependency often deteriorates unnecessarily for systemic purposes. While the center locale finds relief during weekends, holidays, winter, and major political events, dependencies may require subjection precisely when the center locale is not providing it.

In addition to individual consciousness, social dependencies also rely on an individual's peak consciousness. Even if an individual feels the need to disperse from peak consciousness, those who depend on their influence may be left without the proper subjection needed for their development. In such cases, the peak is not the immediate necessity; another momentary propagating influence may suffice. Individual dependencies must, therefore, schedule their development of consciousness according to the predicted availability of the individual upon whom they rely. This scheduling allows them to proceed with their own development so that the peak necessity aligns with the dependency's subjection. When an occasion for dispersion arises, it will correspond with that dependency.

This synchronization is also true for dependent locales that follow the schedule of the center locale. They can predict most of its moments of dispersion—except for unforeseen political events. When these locales learn the schedule of peak and coinciding dispersion, they experience a similar process, aligning with both their own necessities and those of their dependencies. However, when a dependent locale faces an unpredictable political event that diverges from the center locale's schedule, it must disperse even as it loses the timing of subjection. For this reason, the endurance of a dependent locale's necessities—including political inquiries—to be kept to a minimum to prevent disruptive effects.

For individuals, the same principle applies: they should not dwell on moments that would force dispersion, that is, if they are dependent on another individual or structure that is unprepared for such an occasion. Instead, a form of repression is necessary so that when scheduled dispersion arrives, they can address their political or personal matters. For example, it is conventional that dispersion from consciousness subjection typically occurs on weekends. This brands weekends the time when locales and individuals attend to their personal or entity-specific necessities, ensuring their availability for subsequent exposure.

A wintry environment provides an extreme example of cosmic influence upon such subjection. It is nearly impossible for the center to maintain a peak level of subjection during winter, so its dependencies use this occasion for dispersion. When conditions change, these dependencies then move to receive the exposure afresh.

An individual may adhere to either a structural system or an individual, all which is not aligned with the center locale. A primary example of this is childhood, when parental figures serve as the dependencies for encapsulation, often misaligned with the center locale. Children, unable to perceive beyond the parental structure, assume these figures represent the entirety of reality. Consequently, the child immediately notices the parental schedule, making them available to receive exposure when the parents are at their peak; and to disperse when the parents are not.

The child accurately identifies the moments and seasons during which they can access this encapsulation; at other times, they experience dispersion of affairs, using those moments for their personal consciousness development. Ironically, weekends, holidays, and winter become the occasions when the child gains access to parental encapsulation, even though these are the very moments when structural consciousness behaves in an opposing manner.

The Dangers of Overloading Consciousness and Dispersion

A parental figure may maintain peak consciousness during these moments, potentially opposing structural consciousness and remaining in an infantile state alongside their children. Alternatively, there may be a grave misunderstanding: the experience during a weekend or domesticative occasion might be mistaken for peak consciousness, while the external realm on regular days is discounted as not being part of peak consciousness.

This misunderstanding is common across all locales and individuals because, first, the child gains access to consciousness through these moments. Consequently, the child may come to believe—often impressionably—that these moments provide the entirety of consciousness encapsulation. Secondly, the involvements during these interactive domesticative moments are highly seductive, giving the false impression that they represent the peak. However, true consciousness in its full form is not seductive; any seductive property indicates that it has been distilled is indirect material. Seductive properties only emerge when one detaches from consciousness altogether and distills it into a very potable substance, ready for individual consumption.

Parental Role in Conscious Reception

Parental figures play a central role in facilitating a child's access to consciousness. Even if they are aligned with structural consciousness, the child may still be barred from entry and must rely solely on domestic moments during interactive occasions. In this regard, parents create a haven for the reception of consciousness, even if they are not genuinely upon such subjection but are only performing such, allowing the child to form their unique consciousness. If the parent fully engages in subjection, offering genuine exposure, it could overwhelm the child's consciousness, preventing them from gaining access due to their inability as engaging at any level.

Anyone who has experienced an overload of consciousness understands that the psyche cannot endure such high quantities. Instead of absorbing the consciousness, it disperses. While the experience may seem seductive, the child will undergo dispersion when they should be receiving consciousness. This highlights the dispersion process, which—if endured—has a negative effect. When an individual or locale undergoes dispersion, they will not serve as a haven of goodness if they enter subjection while in this state.

Dispersion occurs when one returns to long-standing layers, olden embodiments, or developments that no longer require further enlargement. If they encounter the propagating property, they risk becoming over-actualized, valued more than necessary, and dragging their personhood through systemic parts as though it were the entirety of their being.

Dispersion and the Propagating Effect

Dispersion must occur away from propagation effects, as it is inherent to the process. When an individual is overwhelmed with consciousness, it affects parts of the psyche not intended for such concentrated interaction. Consciousness interacts with the psyche at its identifiable level of sophistication, brushing against the control lines of the individual, and intruding upon areas that are neither prepared for interaction nor adequately developed. This reveals a systemic background meant solely for dispersion.

This is especially evident when a child interacts with a parental figure who genuinely propagates. The child involuntary disperses their underdeveloped parts, bringing them to the forefront even if they are inconsistent with the rest of personhood. In such cases, the parental figure must create a system of consciousness designed specifically for the child's entry, abstaining them from participating in their own encapsulation. They achieve this by charging the instant with their own contextual footprint—serving as oversight for the contextual study. By doing so, they provide a haven without stepping directly into the child's experience, hovering above and below instead.

Structural Dispersion and Regulation

Indeed, it is at the very juncture of the child's initial entry into consciousness that the parent engages in a structural dispersion, a process mediated and regulated by contextual frameworks. When dealing with direct interactions, the parental figure only has a single choice: engage with that process and presume a subjection or appear as they are, even as they remain stagnant in a contextual overlay. To the degree of development in the structural consciousness outside that realm is the degree of necessary context so as not to presume that this seductive experience is anything similar to consciousness.

Dispersion is the occasion in which there is a separation between the peak consciousness and the development of the individual or structural horizon. The very process of dispersion is going to be regulated and controlled by its detachment from conscious subjection. When the effect is a consciousness attachment, all dispersion is not possible—almost as if peak consciousness has arrived and there is no occasion to disassemble and reinterpret parts, for the wholeness has taken effect. Because of this, one will only gain entry into the dispersion when they have succeeded in consciously and structurally detaching from the subjection.

The Role of Detachment and Downgrading

This seems questionable for a central locale in which its entire entity has reached peak consciousness. So, how would peak consciousness itself disperse and enter into its systemic structure and downgrade accordingly? Well, peak consciousness, especially in the center locale, does not have any dependencies above it, so it does not detach but subsides itself, becoming forgetful and ambiguous. The dependent locales can detach by successfully and structurally detaching, waiting for the scheduled dispersion, or engaging in the same process.

Where peak endurance must be maintained in a consciousness flow, one can separate and diffuse consciousness, but the peak will not be able to be maintained continuously. We notice this on the weekends of the center locale, in which it purposefully loses its definition, allowing all havoc to unfold, and no interaction is consequential—almost like a forgetful and lazy individual. We can even say that during these times, the system is fundamentally downgrading due to the perfected effect of disengaging from peak consciousness. However, this is only its humility or willingness for dispersion, despite the definition it gives itself. It is ready to reenter peak consciousness at a moment's notice or when the scheduled dispersion is over.

We can perceive this ability as a detachment from one's existential affairs —as if they were not entirely personal but rather part of a structural position that simply exists. This existential disengagement allows the necessary interaction for dispersion, which cannot occur when one presumes that existential reality is all there is.

Center is afforded its pathway according to its succession. If the center locale does not engage its overarching potential to alleviate its movement and expanse, the propagating effects will be compromised. We cannot expect peak consciousness to maintain a continuous flow because it eventually develops into a state that lacks self-reflection and concurrent processing. Consequently, we will not experience an uninterrupted exposure of the center locale during daily, weekly, or major events; instead, it alleviates the burden of peak consciousness by entering a state that allows the system to process developmental change. Similarly, individual's experience, as their peak consciousness is not noticed or propagating at all times but is a momentary experience when they reach that peak. On regular occasions, they remain within the system of the psyche and internalize the process, so that by definition of internalization, it cannot be a thorough subjection. The individual must do this because the attempt at continuous exposure will be met with stagnation and disruption, as a system that fulfills its task without recognition of its process, so that by definition of the continuous peak, they will not proceed in the necessary embodiment of the lower levels of consciousness, nor will they maintain their grip on the peak consciousness. What we hold onto most dearly is lost from clear interaction. We need a distance from the peak consciousness to fulfill the interaction in its proper form, for a decrepit interaction will hold a diffused formation of consciousness that will assume its improper construction.

Structural Detachment and Dispersion

The same can be said for structural consciousness, where the peak consciousness will not be able to endure a continuous flow but will rather spend most of its routine making sure that systems are intact, ensuring that it reaches its peak for short durations. When they are not enduring the encapsulation, every dependent locale will not receive that real-time receptivity, and thus every locale will be downgraded as the center locale downgrades. The dependency will reluctantly downgrade, often to a further degree of distance that may not be necessary for their systemic interest. While the peak of the center locale will take alleviation at weekends, holidays, aspects of winter, and major political events, the dependency might be in a position where it requires receptivity just at the times when the center locale does not provide it.

To contrast with individual consciousness, we can say that there are social dependencies on one's individual consciousness. Even if the individual finds the need to disperse from the peak consciousness, the dependencies that rely on their influence may be left without the proper receptivity that would ensure their development. For one, the peak is not the current necessity, while another may endure only at this moment of propagating influence. Because of this natural disparity, individual dependencies must schedule their development of consciousness alongside the prediction of the individual to which they are dependent. By having that prediction, they can proceed in their private development, so that the peak necessity runs alongside the receptivity of their dependency. When it is the occasion of their own dispersion, it will be in alignment with that dependency as well.

The same is true for dependent locales, in which they will succeed by following the scheduled process of the center locale, having the ability to predict most of its occasions for dispersion, save for political events that cannot be predicted. When these locales learn the schedule of peak and dispersion, they will endure a similar process of peak and dispersion, so that they will align with their necessity and that of their dependency. This changes when the dependent locale endures a political occasion that is not congruent with the center locale, so that they will require their dispersion even as they lose the schedule of that receptivity. It is for this reason that the endurance of a dependent locale's necessities, even of political inquiry, shall always be kept to a minimum so that disruption does not take effect.

For the individual, we notice the same occurrence: they would behoove themselves not to dwell on the occasion that would have them in dispersion when they are dependent on an individual or structure that is not prepared for that occasion. Rather, a form of repression is in order, so that when the scheduled dispersion arrives, they will utilize the opportunity to deal with their political or personal matter. For instance, it is fairly accepted that there is dispersion on weekends in receptivity, and thus it is the occasion for locales and individuals to take that opportunity to follow their personal or entity-specific necessity so as to be available for the receptivity when it comes into effect.

For a more extreme example, a wintery environment has a cosmic influence on the receptivity. It is near impossible to maintain a peak level of receptivity from the center, and so all its dependencies can use the occasion for dispersion. When that changes, they shall move to the reception of that subjection.

An individual can adhere to a structural system or individual one that is not paralleled with the center locale. The primary occasion for this is childhood, where parental figures are the dependencies for subjection, which may not align with the center locale. Children do not have the ability to perceive beyond the parental structure and will assume these figures as the representation of all reality. Therefore, the prediction of the schedule of parental figures is noticed right away, and the child will be available for reception of encapsulation when the parents are at their peak, and then fall into dispersion when they are in that state.

The child will find with certain accuracy the moments and seasons in which they will gain entry into that encapsulation. In other moments or seasons, they will find a dispersion of affairs and will take the occasion for their own dispersion of consciousness development. There is an ironic formation in which weekends, and especially holidays and the winter season, will be the occasion when the child gains entry into parental encapsulation, even though these are the very moments in which it is the opposite for structural consciousness.

The parental figure can be of a disposition in which they maintain peak consciousness at these moments to be against the very structural consciousness and thus remain infantile alongside their children, or it can be a terrible misunderstanding that the experience endured during the weekend or 'domesticative' occasion is the peak consciousness, while what is endured in the external realm on regular days is not.

This misunderstanding is commonplace in all locales and in all individuals because, first off, the child will gain entry to consciousness via these very moments, hence dictating in a very impressionable format that these moments provide all of consciousness receptivity. Secondly, what is experienced in these interactive domesticative moments is highly seductive, giving the impression that it is the peak. However, consciousness in its full form is not seductive, and any property of such is the very notion of its being non-propagating material. The seductive properties only emerge when one detaches from consciousness altogether and distills it into a very potable substance for consumption.

Parental figures will still maintain the entrance to consciousness for the child's sake, for even if they are aligned with structural consciousness, the child will be barred from entry and will only make do with the domesticative moments at these interactive occasions. This would have the parents provide a haven of reception for consciousness, even if they are not propagating in genuine form but only in appearance, so that the children gain entry into a formation of consciousness. If the parental figure propagates in completion, which is to provide a genuine exposure for the child, it will be the occasion of an overload of consciousness for the child, in which they will gain no entrance due to the inability of engagement.

As any individual who endures an overload of consciousness, instead of the occasion providing high doses of consciousness, the psyche will not endure any of it and would rather disperse from the substance. The experience might be seductive, but the child will be in a process that will have them endure dispersion when they should be in the reception of it. It will rather illuminate the dispersion process, which, if we are to endure, will only provide a very terrible effect. When an individual or locale is in the occasion of dispersion, they will not be a haven of goodness had they entered into the subjection in that state. The dispersion is the occasion where one is systematically entering old parts, old embodiment, and other developments, which do not need to be enlarged whatsoever. If they face the propagating property, they will become actualized as property with more value than needed and will drag personhood through their systemic parts as if it were the wholeness of personhood.

Dispersion must be endured away from the propagating effects, since this very notion is the procedure. When the individual is overdosed with consciousness, it begins to enter psyche parts that are not included for the interaction. It begins to interact at its level of sophistication, brushing along the control lines of the individual. It will pluck and pry into parts of the psyche that are not prepared for the interaction, nor are developed into the ring of the psyche's affairs, illuminating a systemic background that is meant to remain for the occasion of dispersion.

For instance, in familial dynamics, parental figures serve as the primary dependency for children's consciousness. Children lack the ability to perceive beyond these figures, so they adopt the parents as the totality of their reality. In these moments— often during weekends or holidays—the child gains entry into a level of consciousness dictated by parental influence. However, if the parental figure's peak consciousness overwhelms the child, it results in an overload that forces the child into an unproductive dispersion, undermining the developmental process.

9 781971 928142